WALK
with
ME

R.A. NADERMAN

ISBN 978-1-64515-236-1 (paperback)
ISBN 978-1-64515-237-8 (digital)

Christian Faith Publishing, Inc.
832 Park Avenue
Meadville, PA 16335
www.christianfaithpublishing.com

"REDEEMED"
Words and Music by Benji Cowart and Michael Weaver
© 2012 Word Music LLC (ASCAP) and Weave Country (ASCAP)
All rights administered by WB Music Corp.

Printed in the United States of America

DEDICATIONS

Becky: To God Almighty from whom all comes from. To my mom who taught me how to love with the eyes of God.

Aaron: To my Heavenly Father for my savior Jesus. To my children who give me a reason to continue the path.

PROLOGUE

October 7, 2004, it was an unforgettable day, each moment permanently etched in my mind. If I closed my eyes the innermost fibers of my gut would feel entangled in the very moments that compiled the day. If I closed my eyes I could hear the words of that day echo in my mind. If I breathed in, the smell that encased the day instantly swam to the surface of my mind. It was a day that changed me forever, never again would I be the same. If I closed my eyes it was almost as if I could see my soul walking out of one life and into another.

1 Corinthians 2:1–5

"When I came to you brothers proclaiming the mystery of God I did not come with sublimating of words or wisdom. For I resolve to know nothing while I was with you except, Jesus Christ, and him crucified. I came to you in weakness and fear and much trembling and my message and my proclamations were not with persuasive [words of] wisdom, but with demonstration of spirit and power, so that your faith might rest not on human wisdom but on the power of God."

My Promise

Several months into writing this book I found it to be taking twists and turns and sometimes I found myself lost. What direction was this book going in and what exactly did God want me to say? A few months earlier a friend had recommended I read Matthew Kelly's book *Resisting Happiness*. Now it was Lent of 2017, there the book was again, and this time I decided to read it. Sometimes we just need to be ever so grateful for the patience of God and for continually being nudged by the Holy Spirit. Within the very first chapter of the book Kelly poses the question to authors, "What does your book promise?" There was no doubt in my mind that the Holy Spirit was guiding me with that question.

As I looked deep into the message of this book I determined the very focus and promise of this book was that if you take time to get to know someone you come to understand their circumstances and if they become your friend you can love them where they are, no matter how different that may be from your own place or experience. If we come to a place of loving one another where we are, the way we are, then we are loving like God loves us: we are truly living as the body of Christ and that is life-changing and life-sustaining from this life into the next.

CHAPTER 1

∾

LOVE YOUR NEIGHBOR AS YOURSELF

Over and over I have found this to be true of my experience as an occupational therapist. Frequently I would tell people that the favorite part of my job was getting to meet new people daily. And yet it was more than just meeting new people: I was oftentimes meeting them at one of, if not the biggest struggle of their life. Working in healthcare gives you the opportunity to meet people from all walks of life. I had patients who were incredibly poor and at the same time on my caseload would be patients who were incredibly wealthy. I would have patients who had very limited education and yet were extremely wise. I had patients who were over-educated and yet lacked common sense. I encountered people who were optimists even in the grimmest of situations. I met people who had problems that I knew would be resolved fairly quickly and yet so much of my time was spent trying to pull them from a deep depression because they were completely overwhelmed by their current situation. There were those who had toed the line of society, meeting all the desired expectations at just the right times. There were those who had made bad decision after bad decision making their entire life completely challenging because of their choices. There were those who had so many resources and never used them and yet the next person would have extremely limited resources but would have utilized everything they had access to in order to build a beautiful life. There were those who smiled and those who grumped. There were those who laughed and those who cried. There were those who were drowning in guilt and those who accepted their failures and made the best of it.

The challenge for me was always the same: to make a connection and to help them through this time in their life. Sometimes the connection was instantaneous and easy, sometimes the connection was strained and difficult. Sometimes I felt as if I did not make a connection with them until the very last day I saw them, and of course there were some that I felt I never did reach in the way that I had desired.

One thing that was evident, however, was that each new curveball life threw me was an opportunity for me to grow and create a space to understand someone else's struggle a little bit more. The choice was always there, of course, for me to become overwhelmed and draw inward and let those overwhelming feelings stew and brew within. Honestly, as we all fall, I do too, and when I fell into my own "poor me" attitude, turning my attention inward, it always became harder to connect with others. Those around me became annoying and frustrating. But when I took my own situation of frustration, my own life challenges and simply called it that, and remembered that God had a plan for me that was bigger and better than my current situation, I was able to move outside myself and help build up the people around me that I encountered each day.

If we take the time to consciously look at each person in a nonjudgmental way and then truly try to see what he or she has to offer the world, our world will change. When we know someone's situation and we come to find the good in that individual, no matter how hidden it may be, it changes us. That is the great experience of our existence: that our interactions with each other change who we are on the inside. We cannot encounter each other and remain the same unless we put up very big walls to keep others' opinions, ideas, and experiences out of our own. The ridiculousness of that in itself calls us to ask, why would someone do that? Why would we choose to remain the same and not encounter different ideas and different experiences? Is it fear? Is it arrogance? Is it apathy? What stops you from encountering something different and someone new?

In so many ways we want to change the world around us. We each have our own passions and desires we wish were fulfilled. Many poets and musicians over the decades have pointed us to look inside ourselves first in order to change ourselves and then change the world. It often sounds too easy and too simple. Yet on the contrary, changing ourselves is the most challenging. We as human beings cling to our own ideas and beliefs. Looking inside and admitting our own need to change is hard and often painful work. Recognizing our own shortcomings grows our empathy for others because we realize we are not perfect and therefore we shouldn't expect it from others.

As a parent, I often reflect on if I have enough diversity in my own life to provide for my children. My husband and I discuss what our lives look like to our children. Does the way we live our lives reflect the values we want to teach our children? If we want them to be kind, understanding, nonjudgmental citizens of the world do we reflect that? Does our circle of friends reflect that? Certainly, we could give them really great speeches about how to accept others and to love their neighbors as themselves, but would they really remember our speeches? No, what they would remember is our collective lived experience.

Our example will forever be implanted in their minds. If I gave to the homeless person on the street, then my children would learn that is what you were to do and they would also do that. If I gave my children a speech about how bad decision after bad decision led to being homeless, then they would come to judge the homeless as bad decision makers. If when they came home with tears in their eyes because a friend had hurt their feelings or treated them badly, I told them that hurting people hurt others and encouraged my daughters to pray for the person who had hurt them as I hugged them close and wiped away their tears, they would learn that harsh treatment from their friend was less about their own character and more about their friend's current self-image and situation. If I held the door for the Muslim woman just the same as for the blonde woman who looked like me, they would learn to do the same as well.

When I was a child, my mother would make sure that we visited our elderly neighbor twice a year. My sisters and I dreaded these trips to visit our neighbor. The house was stinky, it was boring and we were obligated to eat the cookies that she provided even though we just wanted to get out of there as soon as possible. Why couldn't we just stay playing outside while Mom went to visit the lady by herself? Perhaps these are similar thoughts that still run through my daughters' heads today when we do similar things as a family.

However, those trips to visit my neighbor lady as a child shaped who I am today. The neighbor lady lived much differently than we did: our house was new, our house was clean, and we had lots of visitors coming in and out of our house. Visiting the neighbor lady taught me she was important and that she was my responsibility. I was called to love my neighbor as myself. I was called to be my brother's keeper. I was made to love.

Perhaps it was these lessons from my mother that allowed me to have the strength to walk into an environment that was completely foreign to me: a medium security prison to visit someone that I had never met before.

As you turn the pages of this book and learn the stories of my life and those of Aaron's life, I hope they will bring forth stories from your own life. I hope this story of friendship will open your heart a little further to see the interconnectedness of those you encounter every day, as well as those who are isolated by geography or circumstance. It is my hope that by sharing this story of friendship you will develop a deeper understanding of the unexplainable love that God has for each and every one of us on this small planet Earth.

CHAPTER 2

UNEXPECTED GIFTS

Finding out I was pregnant in the summer of 2004 was an unexpected gift. It was not only unexpected but also a bit daunting when we looked at the months and years ahead. Not only would we have one baby but two, and then two toddlers! We found out I was pregnant with Isabel while we were awaiting the completion of Olivia's adoption. Olivia arrived home in October of 2004 and six months later Isabel was born.

We had spent many years imagining our family and praying for our family to come to be. I had spent over a decade desiring to be an adoptive mom without giving much thought to having a biological child. Isabel arrived as an itsy-bitsy surprise full of joy and the energy to spread it. As our family evolved, Isabel's passion and joy would prove to be a great blessing from God that our family needed to survive.

Sometimes unexpected gifts come in the form of tragedy. Such would be the case for Aaron. For Aaron, tragedy was a culmination of difficult circumstances, many of which he was born into, some that society laid upon him as he took his first breath and the result of poor decisions arising from a lack of direction. When he was sentenced at age twenty-one to twenty-four years in prison, the immensity of loss clouded the view of the unexpected gift. In time, the gift within this tragedy would shine so brilliantly that the loss would be almost unnoticed.

This is the story of Aaron, and though it is a story of tragedy and loss, after you know the whole story, it will be impossible not to see the unexpected gift: an unexpected gift of love that could only be described as infectious.

On October 7, 2004, as joy poured from my heart as I held my eldest daughter for the first time, Aaron was taken into custody and accused of a despicable crime. Just as my life would never be the same after October 7, 2004, neither would Aaron's. I met Aaron in March of 2016, in a prison two miles from my home.

I had spent the last twelve years being a wife and mother. When Olivia and Isabel were one and two we felt called to adoption again, and in 2008 Maria was finally home and our family felt complete. Twelve years of motherhood had brought me joy, exhaustion, turmoil, anguish and love. There were moments when things were rolling smoothly, coasting and I felt proud and successful; but more often than not I felt insecure, unsure and weak. These feelings were the ones that brought me to my knees and kept me up at night. They also were the very situations that brought me straight to Jesus, questioning, confused, rambling and sometimes even speechless. While these had been trying times, I was grateful and felt blessed to reach a place where I could say I had a relationship with Jesus. He was my rock. He was everything to me.

Aaron had spent the last twelve years of his life behind bars, accused of rape, of which he had maintained his innocence the entire time. One would expect that he had spent the last twelve years fighting for his freedom, trusting in the justice system which repeatedly failed him. It was true he had trusted that he would be freed given there was no physical evidence. He had trusted in surveillance video which would turn out to be missing. While it was completely understandable and expected that I would meet a man crushed, hopeless and angry, nothing could have been farther from the truth. Just two miles from my home, I met a man who radiated joy, praised God openly and was full of hope for his future. Aaron was not bitter or spiteful. What was obvious was that Aaron was full of the love of God.

Aaron reminds me often that "God is glorious, holy, patient, merciful and loving. In everything our Father can be trusted. IN EVERYTHING!" It sounds so simple and yet it is incredibly difficult to believe and accept. For me this reminder cannot come too often. If I were to get a tattoo, this would definitely be the one for me to get, TRUST GOD IN EVERYTHING! I questioned again and again, even though God had proven himself to me over and over. What was it that made me second-guess? As much as popular culture would choose to deny it, the truth is that second-guessing God is a result of our sinful nature.

Those questions that make us hesitate and the reasons that flood our mind to not follow God come directly from the only one who wants to keep us away from God. The Devil entices us by utilizing peer pressure and twisting our own intellect in order to talk us out of trusting God. When we do not trust God we are bogged down by the pressure to make things right and to solve problems without God: on our own. And yet, many of us stand and profess on Sundays to trust in God and do God's will. Trusting in God will not only lead to a deeper relationship with Him but it will also produce many unexpected and amazing gifts.

The input from all other sources floods our homes, our families and our minds the rest of the week. It is no wonder that we get caught up and swept away into putting our faith in our own conclusions or the conclusions presented by society. We know where this leads, we have all been there: sitting with our poor decisions, choices that in hindsight look so very ridiculous and that often were really no-brainers.

Let me share with you an example from my own life. In the summer of 2015, my husband and I took our three daughters on a family vacation to Guatemala. This was a very special family trip as two of our daughters were adopted from Guatemala. We returned to our daughters' country of birth to see and experience this beautiful country together. We were ever so blessed to have my mother and my husband's mother and father join us on the trip. As you are likely aware, Guatemala is economically a developing country. Poverty was visible to us every day, at levels that we rarely if ever witness in the United States.

One evening we were walking home from dinner, and I heard the voice of God tell me to give my shoes to a homeless woman who was sleeping barefoot on the sidewalk. Instead of just doing what I was asked, which is really a no-brainer, I pondered in my mind, was that really God? Then all the excuses came flooding in, "What would my in-laws think?" "The road was a cobblestone street and it was dark, what if I cut my foot?" Notice what starts happening in my mind as I get farther from the voice of God: I begin to reason "I need these shoes for the rest of the trip. Yes, I have others but these are one of my favorites." The reasoning that takes place in my mind really gets ridiculously, outrageously, embarrassing.

I wish I could tell you that I rejected the doubts and lies and took shelter in God's command, but I did not. Instead I listened to the voice of doubt, the voice of the Devil. When I tell this story the look of disappointment on the listener's face always hits me. It would be a great story, wouldn't it, if it had a different ending? People often tell me, "Imagine, what your girls would have learned from seeing that?" I think of all the speeches I have given my girls about sharing with others, of putting others' needs first, and yet when God gave me the chance to show them, I said "no, thanks." That is exactly what the Devil is aiming for: a separation between the voice of God and us.

Aaron reveals, "Be aware of the schemes of Satan. As God through the Holy Spirit uses vessels (people) to do his will, speak or act on his behalf, in the same order Satan and his dark angels operate. I've learned the deception is visible, but you must have eyes of the Holy Spirit to see, that vessels or people who have allowed the bitterness and hatred to set in. When you become alone in Jesus, you will suffer! As he overcame, you will too, by faith that is supported by action." In John5:5–9, an ill man comes to Jesus seeking healing. It is the faith that brings him to Jesus seeking healing and once he is healed he picks up his mat and leaves. His faith that leads to healing now leads him into action. Jesus suffered because of sin and when we are alone in Jesus we suffer, too, because we see the sin of the world and we feel the pain of that disobedience to the very God we love."

What if…what if I had have listened to the voice of God? What might my children have learned? Would my husband, mother and mother- and father-in-law have been moved in their relationship with God? How may a pair of shoes have changed the life of the homeless woman? Perhaps she would be able to walk farther to get shelter to sleep the next night. Perhaps she could seek employment or assistance that was too far to walk barefoot. But what if that simple act would have changed her relationship with God? In my choice to ignore the voice of God and listen to the lies of Satan, not only had I denied myself a closer relationship with God but also had likely kept all those who were with me from that same relationship. We must learn to not only hear but trust the word of God, not only for the sake of our own soul but for the souls of those we love most dearly.

CHAPTER 3

UNLIKELY FRIENDSHIP

Did you know that scientific study of the makeup between human beings has revealed the genetic similarity between any two human beings is 99.9 percent? This makes the difference between any two human beings a mere 0.1%. Isn't that fascinating considering how much time we spend recognizing and pointing out the differences between us? As I got to know Aaron the 99.9 percent seemed so obvious: the stereotypes we both fit into faded away and the outward differences seemed insignificant as we got to know each other.

Aaron and I could not have been more different and yet we were cut from the same cloth. I am the oldest of four daughters, raised on a farm in rural Illinois. My upbringing had been carefully sheltered by my parents who were involved in my activities, checked my homework, and researched my friends. During my childhood my parents both worked two jobs, and when they were not able to be with us due to work we were with our grandparents who lived next door to us. Nearly everyone I knew growing up was white, middle-class, living in a two-parent home and Catholic. I attended college and graduated on schedule with a double major. My parents guided me to a career which I would enjoy and could make a living at. I married my high school sweetheart and after six years of marriage we became parents. I was respected in my profession and community. I was a person people called upon when they needed a chaperone for a field trip or an extra hand at church. I participated in the PTO and taught religion at my church. People smiled and said hi when they saw me. People hugged me and told me it was good to see me.

Aaron was the third of five children. He also grew up in Illinois, but within inner city poverty. His childhood was turbulent and unstable. He would learn to provide for himself and look out for himself as early as six years old. He was born to a single mother, who struggled to provide for her children to the point of living in a Salvation Army Mission. Life seemed as if it would improve when the family moved when Aaron was 5, this time to the suburbs. The family had moved because as Aaron recalls, "Mother was on the run from my youngest sister's dad who was very angry and mad. I believe Post Traumatic Stress Disorder (PTSD) set in at that time. This man would jump through windows at wee hours of the night and beat Momma. We as young as three- and four-year-olds would be woken to this chaos and Momma screaming for her life only to wake the next morning to her sleeping in the bed with him." When the family moved to the suburbs, they were given the opportunity to live in a mostly white middle-class neighborhood. Aaron recalls seeing dads playing ball with sons on manicured lawns. He recalls interacting with these families and observing the children drinking milk with dinner.

Perhaps it is the absence of the "little things" that stings the most: the lack of milk, sheets on a bed, and a new backpack on the first day of school. Those of us who have not had to go without these basic items we take for granted often casually proclaim we could do what we had to do to "get by." Would our feelings change if for generations upon generations the "getting by" persisted? At what point does one become resentful? Those who have lived in privilege for generations often grow indifferent to those in financial and social poverty. Perhaps it is also that those who live with the privilege of abundance are so far removed from those in poverty that they don't even know where to begin or how to begin to offer a hand up. It so easily becomes the way it has always been. These emotional barriers are the very greatest limitations that we have as a society on solving the problem of racial tensions and inequities in the United States.

As Americans desiring unity we must be willing to come together to address these inequities and the emotions they create in simple and practical ways. The simple beginning is to accept and own our history and reality of intolerance and that privilege supports the institution of racism. Ignoring this ugly history hasn't worked. It's time to face this demon and bravely look it in the eye and be willing to see the problem through a lens other than our own.

Initially it seemed as though things were improving for Aaron and his family but soon it was a return to the familiar. Aaron and his siblings would be left for weeks at a time, even up to a month alone. He recalls needing to steal just to have food to eat. Reflecting back as an adult, he recognizes that this would have been obvious to neighbors, who never intervened or offered assistance to him and his siblings in the absence of their mother. Of course these neighbors noticed five children alone for weeks at a time! Did they offer a meal, or knock on the door to see if the children needed help? It is, of course, easy to look back and judge. Certainly there is a serious moral question as to why the neighbors of this young family did not intervene beyond a call to the Department of Child and Family Services. Yet this very moral question exists today, why do we not intervene? Maybe there is not a family next door to us in this situation, but most certainly we can look across town in any city in America and find a family living on the fringes. What will we do? Will we uncomfortably watch from afar? Dare we step forward to meet basic human needs in a way that shows dignity and respect? Dare we be the hands and feet of Jesus? While life in suburbia seemed desirable, Aaron recalls that it was when they drove across town to a relative's home in the projects that he felt at home. This was where he and his siblings fit in. So eventually, the family returned to the inner city.

Soon life was spiraling out of control and Aaron was a casualty of the storm. Aaron began dealing drugs in the fifth grade. He had street smarts beyond that of most adults. He became a father at the age of fourteen, unable to provide physically or emotionally for himself, let alone a baby. Aaron's second child was born when he was twenty. At the age of twenty-one Aaron's life took a tragic turn. He was convicted of the ugliest and most deviant of crimes: rape. He was labeled a sex offender and sentenced to twenty-four years in prison. His visitor list was short. He was removed and forgotten. Few people looked at him or thought of him and if they did their eyes condemned him again with disgust. No evidence was needed, the conviction was made and now he was removed.

Praise be to God! God had another plan for Aaron. God was writing a different ending.

As Aaron and I became friends, the stark differences in our backgrounds and upbringings mattered little. The things we had in common became more obvious. We discussed God, religion, politics, our families, and we prayed and laughed together. After a few months we realized our story of friendship which had only come to be by the mercy and love of God Almighty, was a story that needed to be told.

For me, coming from a background of a strong family unit with parents that were involved and in charge, it was hard to imagine being left to care for oneself at such an early age. I had a mother who helped me fill out college forms! In early summer 2017 as I continued to write and do research for this book, Aaron suggested, much to my satisfaction, that I interview his mother. I was glad he suggested it because I had been thinking she would give the insight that I needed. I called her and spoke with her on the phone. She was sweet and pleasant, and we agreed to meet the following day after Aaron's son's high school graduation ceremony. Prior to the call I had not realized Aaron's son was graduating, and, as had been the case for nearly every milestone in his son's life, Aaron would not be there. "Honey, I'll call you tomorrow after the graduation. We should be home by one o'clock," Aaron's mom sweetly told me.

The idea that Aaron would miss his son's graduation was heavy on my mind, but I was excited to meet his mother. My mind churned with questions for her. I waited with patience on the day of the graduation. By 2:30 p.m. when I did not receive a call I sent a text to her phone, asking if it would still be possible to meet. The clock ticked on and no return call or text. Aaron knew we were to meet and I knew he would be disappointed that we were not able to connect. I was disappointed, too, and yet I realized that the topic was likely painful and sensitive and that perhaps Aaron's mom had decided she just couldn't go there, especially on the day of the graduation. In my next letter to Aaron I told him the interview with his mom did not end up happening. I kept it lighthearted and didn't make a big deal of it. I had known Aaron long enough to know that he was likely to feel responsible for his mother's no show. It turned out I was correct. In his next letter to me he apologized for his mother standing me up.

This situation was actually very beneficial for me, as it made me realize what Aaron had experienced his entire life with his mother. She was not someone he could rely on. He could not rely on her to provide for him physically, nor emotionally. Yes, she loved her son, but just as I had observed in working with a variety of families, sometimes a person was only a mother in name. Sometimes you could observe a mother interacting with her children, or more often than not, it was the lack of interaction that was most shocking, because nothing about the interaction looked like a mother and child relationship.

As it turned out, on the day of the graduation not only had she stood up me for an interview, but she failed to go to her grandson's graduation. I thought of how many times my own mother had stepped in for me if I was not able to go to one of my daughter's events. Many times my mom, even though she lived two hours away, would fill in for me, and help me in a pinch. Aaron didn't have this support now and sadly, he never had.

As you can see, it is very unlikely that Aaron and I would become close friends and discover we had much in common with one another. Perhaps even more jolting is that we would meet when Aaron was serving his twelfth year of a twenty-four-year sentence. It quickly became obvious that it was God who had orchestrated our meeting and only God who could have formed each of us into a person available and willing to accept the other. Our friendship was based on our love for our Father. We did not need to be envious or judge; we could peacefully enjoy the company of each other and share what we had in common while appreciating the other's position. It may be easy for an outsider to see that I had much to offer Aaron, and yet I found myself learning from Aaron all the time and being grateful for the wisdom that he had gained as a result of his life experience.

2016 was a very special year because it was a Jubilee year. In biblical terms, in the Old Testament Jubilee year was all about restoring wrong, whether that be debt or seized land. A Jubilee year was a time to celebrate and a time to pray. The Jubilee year was exciting for me especially because it had been declared a Year of Mercy by Pope Francis. What better way to experience the mercy of God than to share it. The Corporal Works of Mercy were a model for how I tried to live my life. The Corporal Works of Mercy encompass how to care for humanity: feed the hungry, give drink to the thirsty, shelter the homeless, visit the sick, visit the imprisoned, bury the dead and give alms to the poor. It was a great blessing for me to work in healthcare, especially in long term care. I had abundant opportunities to live the Corporal Works of Mercy daily. I felt like the one work of mercy I had not been able to live out was visiting the imprisoned.

I began to pray that God would lead me to this work of mercy to visit the imprisoned. While at work one day the topic of prison came up at lunch. This was a subject that is far removed for most, including myself at the time. I noticed one of my co-workers reacting a bit differently to the topic, a bit quieter than most and yet she seemed to have some insight. I quietly asked her if she knew someone who was in prison. She said yes, and upon me asking who she explained her brother Aaron was serving time at the prison right in our town. As the group began to disperse back to work, I quietly asked Tierra how long her brother was in and what he was imprisoned for. She paused and I excused my forwardness, reassuring her it was ok and really not my business. In hindsight, I am surprised that Tierra told me the details as she quietly carries the crosses in her life with the prettiest of smiles. But on this day, she told me that Aaron was accused of rape and sentenced to twenty-four years and had already served twelve. She was quick to tell me he was innocent. My heart broke for my friend: what a cross to carry quietly on her own. As I gave her my condolences, she shared that she was really the only family that went to visit him. She shared that it was hard to get to visit him due to financial hardships and having to make arrangements for her children in order to visit.

In the days that followed, my heart felt for my friend. At the time I did not realize the childhood Tierra had endured and survived; her smile hid it all. The previous summer I had stumbled across the true story of Dominique Green in reading *A Saint on Death Row: The Story of Dominique Green* by Thomas Cahill. The book not only tells the story of Dominique Green, but in it Cahill illuminates the racial injustice and the mass incarceration taking place in our nation which targets the poor, most especially the poor of color. This book not only changed my perspective on the criminal justice system in our country, it made me care about the issue. Isn't that true of most issues? We need to be able to put a face to the story for it to matter to us. The face of Dominique Green was the face that made me realize that incredible injustices within our criminal justice system mattered to me, a white middle-class mother of three.

The story of Dominique Green remains fresh in my memory today. His is a heart-breaking story, in many ways similar to Aaron's childhood: a story of a forgotten child left to raise himself and later falsely accused. Dominique's story drew national attention and he had a strong group of people who fought for him, and yet despite legal attempts to right a wrong, he was executed on October 26, 2004. Yes! October 2004, the very month and year Aaron was arrested, the very month and year I held my oldest daughter in my arms for the first time. The so-called coincidence of these three events in the same month and year would later come to be revealed to Aaron and me that God was most definitely in charge of writing this story.

I purchased the book for Tierra, wrote her a note, and slipped some cash in the card for her expenses on her next trip to visit her brother. I just wanted my friend to know that I cared that she carried this cross. A few days later she received my note and gift and in all her dignity thanked me but said she could not accept it. No matter who you are as the gift giver, the last thing you want is your gift to not be accepted. So quick thinking prompted me to say that she could not refuse my gift because it was not for her, but for her brother and that it would be his decision to make. Done. She accepted and I was happy. What I had not expected was to hear that her brother wanted to write me to thank me.

The thank you note I received from Aaron was perhaps the nicest thank you note I have ever received. My gift of cash which would not have covered dinner for my family of five out to eat elicited a thank you note that spoke volumes. It was a thank you note that even the hardest of hearts could not refuse to respond to, and so began my friendship with Aaron.

You may wonder what he could have said in a simple thank you note that made a difference to me, who seemed to have it all. It was his peace and kindness and gentleness. Certainly not what I had expected from a man who was sentenced to twenty-four years doing time in an overcrowded prison for a filthy crime he maintained his innocence of. After twelve years of living in what I could only imagine as an insanely stressful environment of sparseness, here was a man of peace and gentleness? How could this be? I was intrigued: I wanted to know more. I wanted to know the rest of the story.

After exchanging letters for a few months, I went to visit Aaron for the first time. Prison was as intimidating as I had imagined, but in different ways than I had anticipated. Undoubtedly one would expect the inmates to be a little unsettling to a new visitor, but the authority of the guards was more unnerving. However, above that, on my first visit to see Aaron the overwhelming presence of God was what I noticed most. I must first state that in all my trips to visit Aaron I have found most guards to be quiet and respectful citizens doing their jobs. After waiting for nearly ninety minutes in the visiting room at a table by myself while other tables bustled with conversation, Aaron finally arrived. We exchanged much of the same information that we had relayed in the letters back and forth, sharing our stories and interjecting questions to clarify parts the letters had not explained enough. I had not met anyone like Aaron before: joy and peace radiated from him and he absolutely loved to talk about God. Without a doubt it was his favorite topic. He was confident in the love of our Father and was completely unashamed to share it.

From that point on we continued to exchange letters each week and I would visit Aaron each month. There are certain events in our lives that mark turns and transitions. Meeting Aaron was a milestone in my life, which would not be the same again!

From as far back as I can remember, God had placed a fire in me for social justice. Racism was a topic that I read about, researched, and debated. Given that I have blonde hair and blue eyes, racism is something that I rarely experience personally. When I was a teenager, there were a series of cross burnings that were taking place in Dubuque, Iowa and I lived across the river in East Dubuque. It was not uncommon to wake in the morning to news reports of a cross being burned in the night and windows being broken. It was scary and shocking to think that this was going on in the 1980s and 1990s. With the threat of secretive hate, it is easy to cower in fear and remain restless in anxiety. However, Aaron reminds me that light dispels the darkness. We are the light of the world, and our light must shine to dispel the darkness. Isn't this so true? Once the darkness is exposed there is no longer fear of it. We know what it is, we have a name and we have a face. The darkness wants to remain dark and unexposed; that is where the power of the darkness lies. Therefore, when we, the light of the world, encounter darkness, it is our duty to shine bright to dispel the darkness for humankind. It is not some righteous act, but rather what we are called to be and called to do. Our light is a gift from God. It is a gift to be shared, a gift to shine to light the path for others. My hope is that this book will shine some light onto your path as Aaron has shined his light onto mine.

CHAPTER 4

RACISM IN AMERICA

Most importantly, try to remember that
this isn't the end of the world; it's the beginning of a hard and worthy challenge.
—Unknown

For most of us, the issue of racism in America is complex and
confusing. For some, the issue is foreign: an issue they believe they
rarely encounter. For others, racism is a daily battle that is not to be
spoken of. Racism in America affects each and every one of us every
day. While we accept racism in America as "the way it is," those of us
who profess to be followers of Christ know that racism has no place
in the kingdom of God. If we are all created in the image and likeness
of God, then no one person is better than the next.

Racism in America has been obvious and it has been subtle. It
has been bold and it has been sneaky. It has been taught and it has
been learned. If we look at racism only through our own lens, we
do not get a clear or complete picture. Addressing racism with an
intent to disarm requires a broad lens and an open mind. Racism
in America has a history. It is a player in the present, but it does not
have to have a future.

Many times I believe we are limited by our own vantage point.
We fail to see that while our own position may be true, someone
else's perspective may also be true though it appears opposing. For

example, if I say "I don't see racism in my circle of friends or in my workplace," this statement can be true for me and false for the person next to me, who shares that same workplace with me. While our perspectives can be vastly different they can both be true. It is not hard to imagine someone using the phrase "they are pulling out the race card." If you have not experienced racism in the role of the victim or target, it certainly may seem that someone could be "playing the race card" to achieve personal gain. If, however, for generation after generation you watched as people who shared your skin color had to work harder to achieve the same success as those with lighter skin color, you would be inclined to wonder if the slight from a coworker, for example, was due to your skin color. You may question, what if I was passed over for the promotion because I didn't look like I would blend with the rest of the team in upper management despite my continued high-quality work? The truth is, we do not have to experience injustice to know the face of it. We just have to be willing to listen and consider someone else's experience.

When my daughters were young (eight, seven, and five), I would often take them to the YMCA with me at night. One night I had the oldest two girls with me and I instructed them to walk the track while I sat in the sauna for a few minutes. We were unaware that they needed adult supervision on the track. Suddenly, there was a frantic knock on the door of the sauna. It was my daughter. She was crying and alone. I quickly got out of the sauna and asked her what was wrong. It turned out that while they were walking the track an employee of the YMCA, Joe, had tried to stop them on the track and when they did not stop he walked after them to speak with them to explain they were not to be on the track without an adult. Joe was a friendly African American man who had worked at the YMCA for years He had his name tag on, was wearing the YMCA employee shirt, and I always spoke to him when I saw him. My daughters, however, did not recognize him and ran from him as they were scared and did not know him. One daughter had run to me and the other to the front desk. Joe also came to find me to tell me he was just trying to speak with them. I smiled and thanked Joe, but on the inside my stomach twisted and questions ran through my mind, questions I knew the answers to but didn't want to admit. Had my girls run from him because he was Black? Would they have run if he was a white man? Did I not provide enough exposure, enough diversity to my girls? Deep down I knew my girls had run from Joe because he was a Black man. To me there was nothing intimidating about Joe. He was average size, in his fifties and was always soft-spoken and friendly. The incident with Joe at the YMCA made me realize I needed to re-evaluate the way I was raising my girls. My lifestyle, my circle of friends was not teaching them what I wanted them to learn. This experience was a wake-up call for my husband and me.

Years after the incident with Joe at the YMCA, my daughter commented to me after friends had visited us, "Mom, Lauren is afraid of Muslims." This comment of course surprised me. I asked, "How do you know?" Isabel responded, "Because when we were walking at the park and there was a Muslim woman, Lauren moved away from her and said, "We should go." I was surprised by my eleven-year-old's ability to observe the subtle movements and comments of her friend. If my eleven-year-old daughter made this observation, certainly the woman had as well. Certainly, Joe knew why my daughters had run and certainly it was not his first time experiencing racism in this form. Sadly, these were some first-time observations for me. How often do those of us in the white majority carry on obliviously while those around us suffer the effects of racism? How we treat others and how we react to others is a reflection of how we feel on the inside, whether we realize that or not.

For a large part, institutional racism and white privilege continue to exist due to a passive majority who have given little thought to recognizing when these situations arise in our day to day lives. There is no doubt in my mind that if Lauren's mother had been aware of her actions and comment her reaction would be the same as mine was to my girls running from Joe at the YMCA. When we do not recognize these situations of racism present in our daily lives, it is easy to experience denial or defensiveness and jump on the band wagon of "I was never a slave owner and you were never a slave."

Have you ever had the experience of being the racial minority in a group? If you have not, I highly recommend that you place yourself in this situation. It is incredibly eye-opening and humbling. The first time I had the opportunity to experience being the racial minority was in college. Monica and I worked together and instantly bonded as friends. Monica was from East Saint Louis, a city known to be rough, poor and "ghetto," and as I have stated earlier, I was the farm girl from rural Illinois. Monica invited me out one night with her friends. I don't exactly recall what we did that evening, but what I do remember is feeling insecure and unsure. I remember being referred to by one of the other girls as "the white girl" and while that was accurate, it was intimidating, because it set me apart from everyone else. The experience opened my eyes to what it felt like to be the minority. It showed me that even when I wasn't referred to as "the white girl," I was still set apart. I chose my words a little more carefully. Since that first experience, I make an effort to put myself into the position of being the minority from time to time. For me, it is important to remember what my coworkers and friends experience on a daily basis. I have learned to look beyond words and watch reactions and respond sensitively with compassion and understanding.

In 2015 when we traveled as a family to Guatemala, my middle daughter, Isabel, who is our biological child, was nervous and uneasy upon landing in Guatemala. She wanted to stay close to my side and immediately began to count the days until we would fly home. Thankfully, within three days she was more relaxed and enjoying the trip. Isabel was insecure because for the first time in her life she was in the minority. People turned and looked at her wherever we went. Her silky blonde hair that was bleached nearly white from the summer sun, her blue eyes and petite features drew attention. Meanwhile, Isabel's two sisters seemed to sigh a breath of relief as they experienced blending into the crowd for once. Now, two years later, Isabel experiences being in the minority once a week when she attends a religious education class where she is one of less than ten white children in a group of over seventy-five students. She looks forward to religious education and has no hesitation when the van pulls up to the drop off door to hop out and yell, "Bye, Mom!" Isabel also has eyes now to notice not only how someone who is in the minority may feel, but she is also able to identify subtle racism that many her age and race would not recognize.

Recently I cringed as I read a post on social media that said, "I was never a slave owner and you were never a slave so get over it!" The statement, which upon initial glance seemed true and clever and denounced the "race card" as no longer valid. When I take a deeper look, I realize that indeed I was never a slave owner, but I have without a doubt benefited from the oppression of people of color. I could breeze by unnoticed because the behaviors of people of color were hyper-focused on in stores, in schools, and in every facet of society. You were never shackled with the physical chains of working on a plantation, having been ripped from your homeland and forced away from your family into labor, that is until your fathers and brothers were ripped from your homes and thrown into prisons for minimal crimes that members of my race were able to escape with a lesser punishment. You were never a slave working on the plantation, yet the demeanor that you needed to adapt with authority continued to be "yes, ma'am" and "yes, sir," just to stay under the radar, survive, and be qualified as decent. Of course, there were times when even that didn't work, which was the case in the shooting murder of Philando Castile. You have been a slave to our laws that sought you out and did not protect you. You have been a slave to our design of a way of life. To succeed you would need to follow what we had decided was the correct path for you. We would not consult your opinion, and you would have to accept our version of success and happiness. You would dress like we chose or we would ridicule you. Your hair would look like ours or we would mock it. We would put down your genius rhyming music because it did not match our genre and the vulgarity of your language would offend us, while our own despicable behaviors would be the status quo.

When we stop clinging to our own experiences as the only truth, and instead listen and observe those around us, we allow the power of God Almighty to move through us and teach us. Our eyes can be opened to the truth. When we set our ego aside and humbly accept that we don't have all the answers, we open the door to truth and knowledge.

Knowing Aaron and where he came from helped me understand how he got to where he was. I believe that could be true of each person we encounter. If we took time to really get to know people and to understand their story, our hearts would break for them. Suddenly, solutions to our most drastic problems would become possible. We would not only be able to see solutions, but we would also be able to have the desire to pursue them. Yet this would require that we step outside of our own comfort zone and take a risk to know someone different and to perhaps reconsider our own beliefs. Knowing someone else's story would cause us to approach problems of our society with not only a passion for solutions, but a peaceful desire to love others and truly desire their success. The solution to these catastrophic problems of hate within our society that have run rampant and destroyed so many lives is our ability to do what we do best as humans: connect with one another. It is time that we stand up like the buffalo herd, it is time that we embark upon truly living as the body of Christ.

A show must be really good for the lure of the television to pull me in as I fulfill household chores and duties. It was November of 2016 and my family was watching the National Geographic channel as I marked items off my to-do list. The story of the buffalo herd captured my attention; it was a scene full of tension and the background music raced with urgency. The plight looked hopeless for the elderly buffalo who was being attacked by ten lions. Lions bit at the buffalo's legs; claws tore at his flanks as the lions clung to his back, while still others paced in circles around him. Perhaps the final predictor of his doom was the male lion who had clamped his entire jaws over the mouth of the buffalo to silence him.

Perhaps you are not aware, as I was not, that it is the strength of the herd that is the buffalo's defense. The herd protects and shields against predators. It is the stomping of many hooves that can intimidate even a pride of lions. A small muffled cry came from the lungs of the buffalo. It was small and weak, but it was enough for the herd to hear. Over the hill the herd of buffalo emerged, arriving to the rescue. The lions watched with caution and debated their options. Some of the circling pacers, young and inexperienced, attempted to go after the herd. The elderly buffalo broke free for a brief period of time but the herd was scattering, and he was weak.

Again the ten lions attacked, anticipating their success. Again, the buffalo's cries were stifled by the jaws of the pride leader. The will to survive was deep within the buffalo and he continued to murmur pleads for the herd. The scene was gruesome: the lions viciously took advantage of the vulnerability of the weakened elderly buffalo, even tearing at his anus. Now the buffalo was no longer standing. His fate seemed inevitable, but not to him who believes that his herd would protect him, and so he continued to mutter cries for help. In the distance that which seemed impossible was in execution: the herd had heard. The herd responded with a new determination. Without fear they pressed in on the lions. One by one, the lions began to leave and eventually the presence of the herd intimidated even the large male lion with his jaws around the mouth of the buffalo. The wounded buffalo lay bleeding, struggling to breathe, but the presence of the herd encouraged him and slowly he rose. The herd surrounded him, providing shelter and protection for his weakened body. The lions looked back as they humbly walked away; now the intimidation was theirs. The lions would not even look to capture a calf from this herd.

This story and the visual that is embedded in my memory often comes to the forefront of my mind as I hear tragic news reports of war and bullying of all kinds. I often wonder what if we were as determined as the herd? What if we valued each of our members, even if they were elderly or weak, or appeared to offer little to our herd, as the buffalo herd had done? What if the members of our herd of humanity who were weak and had limited assets to give and share were valued simply because they were human like us? What if we believed in the power of our unity enough to utter a cry for help no matter how soft our voice was?

The solution to racism and hate has always been love. While at times the things that God calls us to do can be extremely difficult, they are almost always very simple. Loving can be very difficult, so difficult that it can almost seem impossible, and yet it is simple. We are called to love. Our Father will provide the grace we need and the courage we require to answer the call.

The racial injustice in America is undoubtedly a complex problem. In order for us to move toward healing it is critical that we gain an understanding of the dynamics that are facing persons of color, most drastically being those in the Black community. Michelle Alexander lays out the history of an unfair judicial system and the laws that support it in her book *The New Jim Crow*. While it would be impossible for me to condense this topic to a few sentences, it is important to realize that the small difference in the prosecution of cocaine and crack, which are the same drug just in two different forms, leads to much more severe punishments for crack than cocaine. This is an important difference because cocaine is largely used by the white community and crack is most prevalent in the Black community. In 2010, historic reform laws were enacted to counter the disparity between cocaine and crack mandatory sentencing laws, yet possession of crack continues to be prosecuted with higher sentences than its powder form of cocaine. Prior to the reform laws of 2010, mandatory minimum sentences were at a ratio of 100:1 for crack vs. cocaine. The enacted reform laws reduced that discrepancy to 18:1. However, considering it is the same drug just in different forms, justice would be served at a ratio of 1:1.

These subtle yet devastating double standards are referred to today as white privilege. Not surprising, it's a term that most white people would rather not discuss. Let's be honest, it is unnerving, disturbing and shameful. It is normal to want to run from that and try to make excuses, and yet it is our reality. We cannot solve problems by hiding from them and pretending they don't exist. When we do that the problem is only compounded. I often see comments on social media about why someone believes white privilege either does not exist or is justified.

Recently, I had a sad and yet interesting encounter with white privilege when my husband and I finally sold our home after trying to sell it for a year. My neighbor came over to say goodbye and since she lived so close she was witness to all the people who had looked at the home. Boldly she asked me, "What color are the people who bought the house?" Not only was this bold because the year is 2017, but it was bold because just thirty feet away my two daughters, who happened to be of color, were playing quietly on the steps! I stumbled over my words, surprised she would be so forward and rude. My neighbor had always been so very kind and sweet to my girls and me. I honestly was not sure of the race of the people who were buying the house. I had already moved with the girls and my husband was showing the house and taking care of the sale. I told my neighbor I did not know the race of the people buying the house. She must have sensed my shock and she stated, "Not that it matters, I mean there are lots of colors that are better than some whites." If I was shocked by the question this last statement nearly left me speechless, I was able to respond, "Indeed!" She then changed the subject to how she would miss us and her voice began to break as she hugged me. As she walked away, I wondered, if my girls were some of the "colors" she referred to that were better than whites? I wondered about the Deacon that had visited her home at a time of illness, was he one of the "colors" that were better than some whites?

It is the privilege of being white that gives one the confidence to boldly ask inappropriate and rude questions. It is the false assurance that the opinions of white people are correct. This has been affirmed generation after generation in all facets of society from government, to employment, to education, to media.

I am very familiar with the various opinions that white people hold on racism in America. I asked Aaron to send me information on racism in America from the Black perspective. I waited with anticipation and a bit of anxiety about what I would hear back.

In writing this book I wanted to hear from the Black perspective on racism in America. This was something I had long wondered about. I was able to draw obvious conclusions, but speaking to my friends of color about racism was a delicate and uncomfortable topic, not only for me, but for them as well. The question I posed was, "What do you want white America to know about racism from the Black perspective?" The following is the perspective of Cordale, a cellmate of Aaron's: "I want white America to know that we as Black men are not stupid to what's going on here in America. As real men (those who are conscious of God's will), we need to start educating the youth of today about the real American dream to be free to worship our Creator and spread that knowledge to our families and communities." It is striking to me that the nearly voiceless man in a prison cell when asked to share his opinion, uses his voice to turn eyes to God. That is powerful and speaks volumes.

A strength I witness time and again is incredible resiliency within the Black community. I noticed time and time again the ability to put on a smile and find an easy laugh no matter what the situation. It is for that reason that when Cordale states, "I want white America to know that we as Black men are not stupid to what's going on here in America," it strikes a nerve. It strikes a nerve for me because we all have the ability to make the best of whatever situation we are in, but making the best of a situation does not mean we are in agreement or are blinded to the injustice.

Aaron expounds on Cordale's statement in response to the question of what do you want white America to know about racism in America from a Black perspective, he explains that the American dream includes the ability to worship the Creator without being judged or disturbed by drugs and poverty. Aaron poses the question for Americans to consider: "Where are these drugs coming from and why into poor Black neighborhoods?" He also speaks of the awareness of "invisible desegregation, because we cannot see equal opportunities." Aaron calls out America's claim to know God when he states, "America you are still segregated and divided, because even though you profess to know Jesus, you do not know Him, you only claim to. If you truly digest the teachings of Jesus and let those teachings rest in your heart, you will treat hate crimes as murder, you will demand solutions that seek input from both the poor Black and rich white." Aaron courageously addresses statements about slavery being over: "to the whites who say slavery is over, nobody is being forced to do labor, this statement makes you sound even more racist, because, you know that on any given day you can hide behind your skin color." "We feel the judgement of America upon us from the complexion of our skin color and not our character."

Aaron describes this knowledge in the back of the mind of a person of color that while a white person can be friendly there is always the ability to slip right back into the hidden persona of white

America if something goes wrong. Meanwhile the person of color remains obvious and still living in the skin of color. Aaron encourages white people who truly know the love of God: "to white people who have the love of God, do not be discouraged by the rejection of Black people, be persistent in your motive and show loyalty in the midst of adversity like the many heroic whites who marched with Dr. King even after numerous attacks on their lives. These are people who didn't abandon the cause when the stakes got higher, because they knew they were called and chosen to the cause; they became the cause. They lived and died for the cause." Aaron closes his statement with a prayer for all who have stood strong and fought for what is true and right despite persecution: "I pray their names are in the Book of Life and that they have the best seat at the Lamb's Supper! Amen." Discipleship has never been easy. From Matthew 10:37–39 we read, "Whoever loves father or mother more than me is not worthy of me, and whoever loves son or daughter more than me is not worthy of me; and whoever does not take up his cross and follow after me is not worthy of me. Whoever finds his life will lose it, and whoever loses his life for my sake will find it." Standing up to racism oftentimes calls us to acknowledge and confront those who are very near and dear to us. While difficult, this is how we begin to tear down the very institution of racism in America.

I will close this chapter with an example of the impact of treating others as we want to be treated and what the world would look like if we looked out for each other, truly believing we were each other's keeper.

It was an unusually warm and sunny Sunday afternoon in February of 2017. The park was packed due to the unseasonably warm 70 degrees. In mid-February in Iowa one would typically expect it to be cold and possibly snowing, most definitely not weather for going to the park and grilling out. The grills were full and we were lucky to get one. We spotted four picnic tables together and quickly settled things down on one, immediately going to the grill to have a place to cook our food. In the distance, a family looked with wandering eyes, scanning for an open spot. My husband happened to notice the family looking for a spot in the very area we were in. Stepping out of his own situation, he spoke with the couple who explained that they were noticing the four tables together, which would have been perfect for their impromptu birthday party at the park for their son. My husband explained that we would only be a short time at the grill and that we could move to a single table not too far away. We moved our things easily and completed our time at the grill. They were able to use the same grill that was still hot to cook their food. In gratitude, they shared their rice and tamales with us which was quite a treat for us, a treat that we were only able to enjoy at a Mexican restaurant. While there was a bit of a language barrier, there was no human barrier between two fathers who wanted to have a nice afternoon with their families at the park.

Any of us who have breathed the free air of this country owe it to our countrymen and women to do our part to heal our nation. Doing our part begins with searching our own heart for prejudice assumptions and inaccurate conclusions. Today in America, mass incarceration is the current primary tool to maintain systemic racism.

CHAPTER 5

HOLY MOLY, NO PUMP FAKIN': GETTIN' REAL AND TAKING ACTION

One of the blessings of having a diverse group of friends is the richness of conversation and the continual learning of a different perspective. I love to learn new terminology that I can incorporate into my everyday vocabulary. Aaron and I each brought our culture-specific version of the English language and it was always a source of humor and learning for us to learn the other's lingo. Sometimes I would google a word he used to get a greater understanding but other times it required a more direct, what does that mean kind of question. Learning how to use pump fakin' correctly in a sentence required some additional explanation! If pump fakin' is new to you, join my clueless club! For me to understand pump fakin' took Aaron spelling it to me and defining it, as well as using it in a sentence. Pump fakin' refers to a move in basketball when a player fakes like they are going to make the shot but then doesn't, but it also refers to a person who is inflating themselves or their story. It refers to someone who brags on themselves or acts phony. So someone who pretends to be something he or she is not is pump fakin'. When I excitedly responded, "holy moly!" Aaron laughed and said, "That's so white girl." I'm pretty sure

Aaron did not add "holy moly" to his vocabulary, but I know I sure enjoyed surprising and stumping people with pump fakin'.

There were times I could use pump fakin' and make a connection with a patient that was hard to reach. Knowing the lingo and how to use it bridged the gap. Suddenly I was more alike than I was different. The point is, that to bridge the gap we need to invest ourselves in getting to know others. We need to know not just what the lived experience looks like on the outside but what it feels like on the inside! That requires us to invest our time.

Wrongdoing can only be avoided if those who are not wronged feel the same indignation at it as those who are. ~Frederick Apthorp Paley.

We have all heard it said that everyone has some sort of prejudice. That is always a statement that makes me want to make a quick escape! EVERYONE! Whew, that is so inclusive, perhaps like me you sheepishly ask, even me? Sadly, but honestly, I think I need to say yes, we all carry prejudice, even me.

When my children were young they attended a school that had a poverty rate of near 80 percent. There were so very many terrific acts of Christianity they witnessed daily. There were also many children who attended the school who came from sparse and desolate homes. It is easy for me to realize, looking back, that many of the children that my girls attended school with were children who perhaps came from homes similar to the one Aaron grew up in. As a parent, you try to steer your children toward friends that will build them up and encourage academic and personal success. I encouraged my children to seek a diverse group of friends. As time passed, I witnessed children who seemed to have limited supervision, very limited. I wondered if they came from safe homes. Sometimes I saw behaviors that were so disturbing, or my girls brought home stories that were so concerning, that I knew the children they were referring to did not come from safe homes. Most times I was not aware of the specifics of the problem, yet the fact that there was a severe problem in the home was evident. Perhaps it was the lack of the parental figure, or a parent with few to no teeth or rotting teeth, clear evidence of repeated drug use. Sometimes it was a child that was so withdrawn that it was painful just to look at him or her. Maybe it was the parent with bloodshot eyes at the school social that reeked of alcohol. In my comments with friends and family about my concerns, I was quick to say I wanted diversity for my kids but "good diversity." Something about that statement always made me feel uneasy, but I used it anyway. Was it really a code word for unruly, slang-speaking children of low income that I deemed low class? And wasn't it true that more often than not, those children were Black? Did I want to pick and choose diversity? Did I want diversity of color, but not diversity of social class? Honestly, I think I have to answer yes. I wanted racial diversity without the multitude of challenges that people of low income faced. Did I have nothing to learn from those who were struggling economically daily? Perhaps I was quick to assume that I had been clever enough to figure out the necessary avenue to be successful. Perhaps I arrogantly assumed that my success was more about my will power and drive, forgetting the multitude of blessings from my Almighty Father.

The sad fact was that I knew better than to use a term like "good diversity." Wasn't it a code word like "alt right"? In college I opted for an opportunity that should be mandatory: I elected an African American Studies class to fulfill my history requirement. I knew the history, I knew the truth about what had happened and continues to happen to an entire race of people in this country and still I used the term "good diversity."

Racism in this country has invaded all of us. For some it's blazingly obvious and for others it's a hidden bias. The point is that it is there. If we don't acknowledge it, we cannot heal it. Racism is the cancer that is killing our peace, stealing our safety and multiplying our suspicion.

While having a conversation one day with a friend who is Black, she confided to me that she was hesitant to reveal to people that her children were biracial because people were not accepting of that. By "people" she was referring to Black people. I was shocked. I had long known that this was not always looked on favorably in white circles, but I did not realize this was also true of other races. Obviously, that was a judgement from my own position of white privilege. Yet it also pointed out that racial judgements were not limited to the white community.

The time is now for us to get real about the elephant in the room. It's time to call it out, with love and forgiveness and honesty. It is time to take the hand of a friend or family member and lead them to the "other side." It is time to ask ourselves, when was the last time a person outside of my racial group was in my home? How many people in my contact list belong to a group other than what I claim to be my own? I know the excuses well. I've heard them repeatedly and they have rumbled around in my head too. "I have nothing against Black, Mexican, Asian, Muslim, Jewish, Gays. They just don't have the same interest I do" "If they lived here or worked where I do I would be nice to them; I just don't have them in my circle." "If they did their part and didn't drain the system, then I could understand." Can we all agree that these statements are not only wrong, but invalid? In some way or another, all of the above statements remove our responsibility and push the responsibility of a diverse society back on the people who are not in our circle.

Consider a time when you were new to a city, job, school or group. Recall a time when you entered a situation where you knew no one. Now consider how confident you were to integrate. Likely, someone approached you and showed you the ropes, smiled at you and made you feel less awkward. The white majority has a responsibility to actively address racism with actions and words: not just to support movements toward racial equality but a responsibility to lead. The white majority is in control of finance, government, education and institutions. It is time to be in control of dissolving racism and xenophobia.

Here are some practical ways we can work to be part of the solution:

Stop the thought! The next time a statement grouping an entire group of people is made, stop your thoughts in action and dare to consider another perspective. Then do that a few more times, gain confidence, ask God to lead you to truth, and then ask God to give you the courage to open your mouth and speak the truth. Maybe you begin with a simple question like, "Why do you think that"? This puts pause to the person making the statement and those around also may begin to consider something different than the status quo. Sometimes a bolder approach is necessary: "Oh, I don't agree with that."

Put yourself in the position of being in the minority. This is something that should be practiced regularly. Being in the position of the minority keeps us humble. It gives us perspective and trims our sails, all things we need regularly. When you experience being the minority, it changes how you view the world and how you react to those you encounter who continuously live as the minority.

Seek relationships with those from different racial and social and religious groups. As in all things, ask God to lead you. You will be amazed at the people he gives you! The power of the words "those people" can be removed by the face of a friend.

Begin with action even if it feels uncomfortable and stay with it until it is comfortable. This can be the case when we consciously place ourselves in the position of being the minority. Read an article or a blog with a different point of view than your own and challenge yourself to see the other side. Open yourself up to listening and not judging someone else's perspective. Social media allows us such opportunities constantly. For all the bad rap that social media gets, this is one benefit of social media that can truly help us to grow. An interesting example of this is a social media group I belong to as a transracial adoptive parent. This particular group was started by adult adoptees who were raised by parents outside their racial group with support from white parents raising kids of color. White parents requested permission to join the group and adult adoptees of color agreed to share raw and painful past experiences. This was done in an attempt to educate white parents about opportunities to create a culturally nourishing environment, with the goal of each new generation of transracial adoptees being culturally confident in their own skin. The group also included professionals who had worked with both adoptees and parents such as social workers and counselors. One would think that there would be mutual respect and admiration for a desire to learn, and gratitude for sharing from a vantage point the parents would not have otherwise had. I believe this is the intent when parents join, yet when beliefs get challenged oftentimes there is push back from white parents with sensitive feelings who refuse to accept an adoptee's lived experience. Adult adoptees of color nearly always expressed gratitude for their white adoptive parents and prefaced statements with the belief that their white parents had done all they could for them at the time with the knowledge they had. Yet when the adult adoptees cautioned white parents that it was not good for their child of color to be raised in near whiteness or total whiteness, parents would respond with hateful words in an attempt to dismiss the recommendation. Parents would make excuses as to why they did not fit into that category, why their particular actions were okay, and attempted to silence the adult adoptees or put them in their place. These situations always proved to be great examples of white privilege: an absolute confidence that the white point of view is correct and that there is an unspoken duty to put a person of color in his or her place and let them know they were wrong in their thinking.

> Love is the only force capable of transforming an
> enemy into a friend. ~ Martin Luther King Jr.

The topic of racism isn't a desirable or comfortable topic for anyone, those of the minority or majority. Yet it is a topic that demands our attention.

CHAPTER 6

BREEDING GROUND FOR SELF-DESTRUCTION

Shortly after meeting Aaron and learning of his story, I realized that while his story was shocking to me, it was not an unusual story. In fact, sadly, it was an incredibly common experience. Aaron's story was a story well-known to the Black community. To be Black in America meant to know someone behind bars.

A common misconception is that "this is America, we all have the same opportunity." It is true that we live in the land of opportunity, but not all of us have the same opportunity. The blows to the Black community have gone on for generation after generation. They have moved from being blatantly obvious to calculated and subtle. I believe we cannot fix other problems of our society without fixing this problem. This is a bold statement, I know, but as we consider the continual assault to the Black family unit we see the unraveling of the safety net for too many children hoping for a brighter tomorrow. How can we expect a change when we have a cycle of broken families, fatherless families, and tragic numbers of abortions scarring souls while stealing hope?

Aaron explained something to me that I had never realized, which is that Black children living in this hostile and oppressive environment become not only angry and have hatred for the oppressors, but, even more damaging, they can develop a hatred for themselves.

Self-hatred breeds self-destruction. We have all heard and likely experienced "misery loves company." Can't we all recall grumbling as children and, even more regrettably, as adults, with fellow classmates or coworkers when we feel disadvantaged? Aaron recalls "For me growing up in project housing, all I saw and heard was poverty-stricken people, who fought, stabbed, shot and robbed one another, because of self-pity and deep pain and hurt, because of the injustice and decree that has been spoken over Blacks' lives for generations. The message that we are caged animals needing segregation from the privileged white population." This is the privileged population that lived in the suburbs with manicured lawns, drinking milk with dinner. To Aaron, the grass across town undoubtedly looked so much greener. The houses were spacious and neat and two cars were parked in the driveway, one for the mother and one for the father. How would a young boy not want to have that which seemed worry-free, but more importantly, safe and pain-free? Of course, it consumes the mind of the youth in this circumstance to be hyper-focused on how to achieve all that he was lacking materially, emotionally and socially as quickly as possible. Is not self-preservation an innate characteristic: survival of the fittest?

And so, Aaron's bright but traumatized mind began to frantically search for a remedy. He kept his eye on the prize and used the skills he was taught to achieve the things he desired in life. Aaron was not only born to a single mother, but to a woman who had been a teenage runaway; a runaway who had found safety within the protection of the gang. The sacrifice of her morals, which she needed to do to sell drugs, seemed like the necessary evil to safety and survival. Perhaps she managed her inner turmoil or soothed her frayed nerves with the very drugs she was required to sell. A small price it seemed initially, to have the safety of four walls and food on the table. Did it seem like a temporary solution to a greater problem that turned into a monstrous addiction?

As family life spiraled out of control, of course the inevitable would come to be: the call to the Department of Child and Family Services, known as DCFS. Relatives looked on and could not take it any longer. Something had to be done and so the call was made.

Aaron then found himself, as he describes it, "sleeping in an unfamiliar bed which would scare me and cause me anxiety and more pain." This fueled the fire of PTSD in a young child who didn't know the term, much less understand it.

As Aaron grew older, so did his frustration and anger with being a victim to a circumstance he was born into and had no control over. Even if he couldn't articulate it, he desired to have a parent, in fact two parents, who would protect him and seek his best interest. The weight of this burden lay heavily on Aaron's shoulders. He wiggled and squirmed to escape this life. He carried emotions too heavy for even the adults in his life to manage, much less a child who was also responsible for meeting his basic needs of food and shelter. Life was uncertain. There was no one to depend on. For these reasons, it is not surprising that teachers and school staff found Aaron to be behaviorally disturbed, leading to him being placed into an isolated class for those with behavior disturbances.

Aaron's parents struggled with demons of their own, preventing them from being the parents their children needed. Aaron was the third son born to his mother and father. His parents' turbulent relationship allowed Aaron's father to believe for most of his childhood that Aaron was not his son. Aaron recalls his father showing up with Christmas presents for his siblings but not him. How devastating that must have been to a wide-eyed child eager with anticipation at Christmas. Aaron's father lived the gang life on the streets selling drugs and gang banging. He would come in and out of Aaron's life, but was never constant, never dependable. Vivid memories from the age of seven come to Aaron's mind with clarity of his mother's addiction to crack cocaine. He recalls the Pepsi can sitting on the table with holes in it, his mother pacing all night long and the terrible smell would forever be etched in his memory. Her addiction would lead to her disappearance for weeks at a time. The anxiety and anger would only be further fueled in Aaron. There was nowhere to turn for help. Those around him, neighbors, struggled with the same challenges, and those who didn't were simply too exhausted and did not have the resources to intervene. Who would love this broken, angry, scared little boy? There seemed to be solutions of consequences for actions, plans to address behaviors, but who would pull him close and offer to wash his clothes and make his dinner?

Today, Aaron is gentle and peaceful with a lot of passion to live life to the fullest doing the will of the Father. He has the clarity of wisdom and of time to be able to look back on his childhood. His description is sobering: "Just imagine this: gunshots morning, noon and night. Fighting, cursing, lying, stealing, robbing, fornicating, babies out of wedlock. Hateful words being said to one another. Mother and Father act as if they are not Mother and Father, this all before five years old. At five you are quoting gang lit because it's being taught to you. You are being molded into a mad man, being policed by people who do not understand your way of thinking. They cannot relate, so how could they find a solution?"

Aaron goes on to add, "It's no wonder you see the shootings of young Black youth and Blacks (in general). What they don't understand is that Black men running from a gun held by a white man, it's engrained in Blacks' minds that white men shoot and kill Black people." These sobering accounts justify the diagnosis of PTSD. I wonder how many other Black men in prison would give the same account. My mind flashes to the challenges our teachers face each day. Certainly the majority of educators are white. Do they understand these dynamics? Even an understanding of the dynamics does not lead to a solution. Nevertheless, as Aaron points out, an understanding of the situation is the first step toward finding a solution.

When life got too chaotic, Aaron's siblings would go to live with their father's relatives. However, since Aaron was unclaimed by his father, he would be left to tend to his addict mother. Every child loves one-on-one time with a parent, even if that time is consumed with bad habits and wrong lessons. Aaron grew close to his mother. He recalls watching soap operas with her. By the time Aaron was ten, his mother's addiction completely took away her ability to parent, and so Aaron went to live with Madea, his maternal grandmother. Madea loved Aaron dearly, but the temptations of the flashy street life had already pulled him in. He was now running drugs for relatives and living a life out of his control. He was smoking marijuana and by twelve- and thirteen-years-old he was shooting guns at people and robbing. The world of the gang now had a firm hold on him. When at fourteen he heard the rumor he was a father he did what he knew fathers did: run. The news of being a father hit Aaron deep but he stuffed it deep in the pit of his stomach, not even sharing the news with his Madea.

Aaron recalls with clarity the day he realized that he did not belong in the isolated behavior disorder classroom. He says he remembers looking around and saying, "I don't belong here." As he transitioned to a young man in junior high and high school he had a variety of support systems: teachers, coaches and his aging grandma. He would continue to bounce from his mother's home, his grandmother's home and even lived with a teacher for a few years.

Life changed yet again and this time the future looked bright. Aaron was chosen to attend a high school in the suburbs. His quick reflexes and natural athletic talent would shine in sports, especially football, and soon he was a star. He remembers feeling very different from his friends with their two-parent homes where meals were shared around a table and milk was served. Successful white suburbia life was a lonely place for Aaron. He not only lacked the two-parent home but the guilt of his success while his family struggled on the streets weighed heavily on him. How could he truly be happy and succeed without his family sharing his success? Aaron writes, "I could never be successful without my family being out of poverty and the addictions and the PTSD being healed."

The scars of his childhood seemed to shatter all prospects of normal stable relationships. Aaron describes his relationships, especially with girls he dated, as being overshadowed by paranoia and attachment issues that developed as a result of his traumatic and unstable childhood. He is quick to tell me that this is very common in the Black community. Certainly he is not alone. He explains that abandonment issues took hold in his case when his mother was distracted and absent due to her drug addiction. In Aaron's case, his grandma stepped in to raise him, yet she was not his mother. He realized that his grandma was raising him because the people who were supposed to could not, due to his mother's addiction and his father's incarceration. Sadly, Aaron explains that over time he learned through interactions with friends and TV shows that in other households, family life is the focal point, something which his own transient household did not have.

This awareness created instability and uncertainty for if you cannot depend on your parents, then you learn early on there is no one you can trust. Aaron goes on to explain how the wounds and trauma from the parental relationships spilled over, infecting all other relationships, most especially relationships with girls. "When young ladies showed me heartfelt love I would find every way possible to mess it up because truly deep down inside my soul I was wounded and traumatized by the woman who was supposed to show me love (my mother) and the man who was supposed to give me an identity (my father) who left their post for a life of crime and drugs or that they themselves are repeating a curse of what also happened to them."

One particular relationship comes to Aaron's mind, a high school sweetheart with a kind and loving heart, whom he dated for two years on and off. She was kind and gentle but even that could not squelch the pull of paranoia of being abandoned. She was beautiful though not the most popular so she was a good match for Aaron who appeared to be a confident jock on the outside but was actually somewhat shy, struggling to sort out how to fit into the mostly white suburban school. As Aaron describes it, "I could be very shy and appear confident on the outside, but having the poverty, abandonment, crime and drug-infested neighborhood experience stains your soul and affects you more than you know. Once you are outside of this trap you realize there is a whole other life experience outside of this in the United States." Aaron describes that he would always find a way to leave before he was left and so their relationship was one of breaking up and getting back together. It was nearing Christmas and she was excited to give the gifts she had bought for Aaron. Aaron found himself in yet another home, financially very limited, and unable to buy a gift for his sweetheart. To avoid the embarrassment, he broke up with her. The cycle of breaking up and getting back together would end this time and she started to date a fellow basketball teammate of Aaron's. As teenagers do, moves are made to get at the one you love, like dating a fellow teammate. Nonetheless

Aaron and his sweetheart were talking again and setting up for getting back together. No one could have anticipated that the teammate would suddenly die of a heart condition during an open gym. The loss would be almost unbearable for a young teen who did not have the security of home to depend on, especially since this followed the tragic death of two cousins on two separate occasions due to gang violence. As Aaron reflects back he says, "I just ask everyone and anyone who is reading this to be sensitive to those who are in need of healing of all types. Don't be quick to judge, but rather, seek understanding and a solution." He pauses and reflects further in an apologetic gesture to the women he had been in a relationship with, "I was wounded and paranoid of you leaving me. That feeling really sucks, especially coming from your mother and father."

Soon Aaron would learn that no amount of success or money could heal his wounds but it was only by the Blood of the Lamb that he could be free of the demons and be made whole. The time for Aaron to be washed clean in the Blood of the Lamb was not yet to be. Today, Aaron can stand with confidence, "Thank our loving Father in Heaven who has a restoration plan. Receive it today!"

When he felt alone and confused, the familiarity of the streets was always there. As his sports talent became known, he was offered college scholarships and moved to Chicago to play college football and study. Life was looking up! Soon familiar struggles would emerge when a friend who was paying his rent did not come through with the money. Without a place to stay, he returned to the familiar neighborhood to earn some fast money. Aaron recalls running into a college friend at a bar one night. The friend pleaded with Aaron to return to college, but the thick wad of cash in Aaron's pocket promised to give him everything he desired. From what Aaron had seen, those thick wads of cash bought nice clothes, fancy cars and a life he had only ever dreamed of.

So at the age of twenty, Aaron was a father of two children and engaged to be married. His twenty-first birthday was in sight and he had plans for his life, plans that included having the family life he always dreamed of. He continued to strive to accomplish this dream by selling drugs. His future was abruptly ripped from his grasp on the morning of October 7, 2004, as he was cuffed, booked, accused and found guilty, then stuffed into a cell to be forgotten. Aaron was accused and found guilty of rape, without the presence of physical evidence. It was one woman's word against his. Here was a twenty-year-old thug who had thrown away his scholarship, returned to the streets and now he was violent. It was easy for the all-white jury to find this thug guilty. While prison was new to Aaron, it was not new to his family. Both of his parents had spent time in prison on multiple occasions. Later, his brothers would experience incarceration and so would his cousin and step-father. Aaron was sentenced to twenty-four years and while it was not a life sentence, it was certainly a very devastating sentence for a young man who had showed so much promise just a few years earlier.

When it came to what really mattered, Aaron and I had so very much in common. Seeking the kingdom of God was continually our hearts' desire. We defined ourselves as children of God. We were each energized by our friendship and had deep respect for each other. We loved to share a good laugh and pray together. We shared with each other how God was speaking to us and working in our lives. We celebrated each other. Jesus had transformed us and we would never be the same after that initial encounter with our living God. We were united in Christ and we had been blessed enough to realize it.

The difference between despair and hope is faith. Sometimes I wanted to kick and scream and throw a fit and tell God it wasn't fair and pout about the fact that Aaron had been dealt the life he had. I wanted to plead on his behalf that God would have mercy and release him, save him from the demeaning authoritarian system he was held captive in. It was easier to pout and be mad at God than to accept that what Aaron was born into was a result of sin. Sin was so overbearing, why wouldn't God just ride in on a white horse and save the day? Couldn't God have molded Aaron into who he was in a softer and gentler way? And yet, I knew that God was the reason Aaron was a treasure to have as a friend. It was God who orchestrated our meeting each other. It was God who had smoothed my rough edges to humble me to be able to see Aaron as a friend. It was God who had been faithful and never abandoned Aaron. It was God who had preserved his bright eyes and easy smile. As a child is physically exhausted after a tantrum, now I had nothing other than to ask my Father to hold me and console me because what was breaking my heart had already broken His. He understood and now I did too, because I was sharing in the suffering of the Father. Our Father's heart aches like that of the father of the prodigal son, because He is that Father. Now, could God help me understand the pain of an aching heart for the soul who refused Him?

CHAPTER 7

IT'S NOT FAIR: THE CYCLE AND EFFECTS OF MASS INCARCERATION

IT'S NOT FAIR! This is the cry of injustice for the young. As we age we learn to "suck it up," "move on" and make lemonade out of lemons. Yet still, even the practical, analyzing adult brain cannot deny the vast inequities within our world.

Whether it be the leftovers rotting in my fridge and the bloated stomach of the starving child or the less noticeable privilege of one group in our society to stroll with ease while another struggles to achieve, the disparity is there. There comes a time when we can no longer say "suck it up and move on, everyone has problems." It is at that very fork in the road where we make the decision to stand up and say "it's not fair and I can see it and I will no longer deny it" or we ease our inner discomfort with the rationalizing that the unfair situation really is fair in some twisted way, and blame the victim. To be silent is to agree. That bears saying more than one time: when we are silent we condone what is being spoken or being done.

In 2015 such became the case yet again with racial tension in the United States. We could no longer with a clear conscious rationalize the deaths of Michael Brown, Freddie Grey, Sandra Bland and Tamir Rice. It could no longer be rationalized as someone just being in the wrong place at the wrong time. When attempts were made to rationalize and blame victims, the video footage could not dispute reality and so the Black Lives Matter movement was born in 2013 in response to the acquittal of Trayvon Martin's murderer, George Zimmerman.

Many people were aware for a long time that "it wasn't fair." In 2008, when Barack Obama was elected to the Presidency of the United States, we wanted to believe that racism, which had become the ugliest of words, was behind us. Perhaps our desire to finally put racism in our past that clouded our view. While it was true that the election of our first African American president was a turning point in our history, the chapter on racism was not closed.

White privilege is the fuel that feeds racism. It is sneaky, smug and acceptable. It is so much more comfortable to say, "This is America, you can achieve anything if you set your mind to it." It is so much more comfortable to look at the world and judge it from your own vantage point. To say, "well, if you weren't in the wrong place at the wrong time" is to dismiss and therefore remove any guilt you may have. It is impossible to reconcile in your conscience a twelve-year-old boy being shot when he has a toy gun. We either need to admit that we have a serious race injustice in our society or we have to dismiss and blame the victim. If we, with prudence and courage, acknowledge the injustice, then we must act. Our soul cries out for a response. We cannot fix the other problems of our society without fixing this problem. Why? It's a cycle of broken families; fatherless families; tragic numbers of abortions scarring souls and stealing hope; generations of partial families without direction, searching for sources of leadership. This problem first began to take root with the inception of slavery, was fostered by segregation and fueled into catastrophe by white privilege. This is not a problem for the Black community to solve alone any more than it is a problem to be blamed on the white majority. This is not a problem that rests with our police officers any more than we place blame on skewed media representation. This is a US problem and it will take us all to solve, all of us to come to the table humbly with hearts ready to listen and hearts carrying compassion. We must begin walking beside our brothers and sisters and not away from them.

Soon after I got to know Aaron it was impossible to not acknowledge this injustice. Initially there was the injustice of false imprisonment, the loss of thirteen years, his loss of parenting and his children's loss of a father. Yet it went so much deeper, including the loss of decisions, and access, and possibility; the denial of human touch from a loved one; the limiting of contact with anyone who knew his past or knew him as a child. That had all been stolen from Aaron for thirteen years and was scheduled to continue for another nine. I soon learned that even after his release he would not be free. Never again would he have the opportunities that most of us enjoy without a thought. As a felon, he would not ever have the right to vote. Where would he live? After all he would have to register as a sex offender. And who would hire a felon and a registered sex offender? Even if Aaron were to be deemed not guilty of these atrocities, he would never have a shot at a normal life again. Not only was that heartbreaking since he was now my friend, but it was unacceptable, because nothing about that seemed like rehabilitation, which was the purpose of our criminal justice system, wasn't it? Didn't we all believe that after "you did your time" you had another chance? Certainly that is what we would choose to believe if it was our own child, brother or father. Didn't we sentence people to prison so that they could "think about what they had done" and "make a better choice next time?"

One would argue that is the very point of prison to deny, to limit, and to punish. Our country has always maintained that the point of prison is to rehabilitate, and yet clearly statistics show that is not the end result. This would leave one to wonder if rehabilitation is really the desire or is the goal to silence and to extinguish? Certainly the skewed diversity represented within the walls of the prison would speak a different language: a language that would tell the story of oppression of a targeted population, disadvantaged by poverty and thrown into a legal system that they were taught was fair. However, upon encountering this system, this targeted population would find legal representation that was inadequate, non-existent or impartial and a legal system that catered to the wealthy and educated. Aaron's childhood story tragically demonstrates this inequity.

The deprivation of prison seeps beyond the walls, beyond the fences, beyond the barbed wire. The deprivation of prison seeps into the lives of those who suffer the loss of a loved one behind that fortress of isolation. It goes beyond the obvious deprivation of a child from his or her parent, a parent from their child, a wife away from a husband. The deprivation is a deprivation at the deepest level of emotional love: the deprivation of comforting another. Having a loved one in prison goes beyond the obvious loss of ability to share time and space with someone you care about. Having a loved one in prison means that you now carry that cross with them.

Sadness was in the air. The clouds seemed to be frowning and the raindrops hung in the air, refusing to be released, like tears boiling below the surface but unable to escape. How often I felt like this about Aaron, and I had only known him a year. What about all those other families? What about all those children? What about all those mothers? What about all those wives? What about all those people who waited years and years and years, perhaps people who waited a lifetime, knowing that their loved one would never be released. Whether the crime was done or not, whether the system was just or unjust, either way the sadness was the same. If there was injustice, there would be anger, of course, but still the primary feeling would be sadness over a huge loss: a loss that remained unspoken, a loss that was a social taboo; a loss that was shameful. Who carried these burdens? Was it your neighbor? Was it the person who sat next to you in the pew on Sunday? Was it the person who sat in the cubicle next to you? Was it the person who cleaned your floors? Was it the person who checked you out at the grocery store? Was it the person who cared for your child as you went off to work? There are so many suffering individuals, all silently holding back their tears like raindrops waiting to be released in the desert.

We all want to make our loved ones' lives easier and more enjoyable. There are such severe limitations on doing that for someone who is in prison. It goes beyond the simplicity of being able to comfort and ensure the person that everything is going to be OK. It goes beyond the limitations of physical contact, which is not only a punishment for the person in prison but also for the family of the one who is imprisoned. Yet as adults we can somehow try to accept and understand the reason. When my mind turns to the children of those incarcerated, the punishment laid on these innocent children is almost unbearable. The idea that the child is not able to be held by the parent is a very severe punishment to a developing child. Dare I even say that it is abusive and neglectful to deprive a child of the loving arms of a parent? How dare we do this?! We are smarter than this, we know the research, we listen to the psychologists, and we believe it because we hold our own children in our arms. We know the importance of bonding and attachment. There isn't one of us who would knowingly withhold it from our own child. And yet, somehow we feel it's justified to deprive the child of the loving embrace of their parent, as a punishment to the parent. Who are we really punishing? The answer is obvious. We must accept responsibility for the role that we play in the emotional scars we place on children of those who are incarcerated.

Of course, we need punishments for crimes and punishments that are deeply felt. This is required in a civil society. Could we make changes to visiting rules that would allow an incarcerated parent to hold a child on their lap? While this issue may be far removed from your circle of friends, it is all too common an issue facing Black children in America. Looking at Aaron's childhood, certainly being held by his incarcerated mother could have only benefitted him.

Mass incarceration is the current primary tool to maintain systemic racism. Mass incarceration not only locks up men of working age, disabling them from providing for their families, it also permanently suppresses the financial status of the entire family unit. Incarceration is not simply a temporary hold on a person's life; it is a permanent change of course. The label of convict remains to limit opportunities in employment and housing upon release. Former convicts are often left voiceless as they are permanently barred from voting. Children are left without parents to supervise them and provide a role model for them; while curtailing their dreams and squelching their sense of security. Youth learn early on, harshly, that the young man of color must walk a very narrow path. Not only does the knowledge of a different standard limit one's dreams but it also serves to create a sense of fear. Families struggle financially to provide while a source of income has been removed and at the same time they have the burden of financially providing for the incarcerated family member.

Perhaps the most devastating effect of mass incarceration is the illusion that justice has been served. We can comfortably settle back in our cozy seats and shake our heads that it is a sad situation, a young man going to prison, but we can remain comfortable because we believe there is a wrong that has been committed by the incarcerated. We can even acknowledge that mistakes will be made, but that most prisoners are guilty. We can only look at mass incarceration this way if we ignore a judicial system that caters to the citizens who are educated and have access to financial resources, and if we ignore corrupt policy.

CHAPTER 8

BODY OF CHRIST

On my visits to see Aaron, oftentimes I would see babies who were small enough to be in baby carriers or car seats. It always tore at my heart to see this little innocent child who was oftentimes laid on the table so that the inmate could look at the child and perhaps touch the child's hand, but never pull the child to his chest to offer comfort, bonding, and love at the deepest level. It always made me wonder what holding a child would do to an inmate who was experiencing deprivation of care and compassion. How would holding a child impact the general environment of the prison? Could holding your child on a four-hour visit decrease the anxiety that this deprived environment elicited daily? Could holding your child on a four hour visit provide enough encouragement to withstand the deprivation for another month or two, or six, whatever it may be? Could holding your child remove the edgy anger that boiled just below the surface?

So again, this environment begged the question: was prison about punishment or rehabilitation? And how many needed to be punished and who needed to be punished? Would those making the decisions about how to punish and whom to punish make the same decisions for punishment for their own families? It is a question worthy of every voter entering a voting booth. In fact, it is a question worthy of every person who professes to be a Christian, because a true Christian believes in the body of Christ and our interconnectedness. If we truly are the body of Christ, then we not only care about those who are incarcerated but also those who are affected by incarceration, at perhaps the deepest level, the children of those incarcerated.

This yet again was another piece of Aaron's story. Aaron came to life in the gang not just because it was in his neighborhood or somewhat in his family. He came to life in the gang not just because his uncles and cousins and older brothers were a part of it; he came to life in the gang because both of his parents were entrenched in this lifestyle. Perhaps he came to life in prison because both of his parents spent time incarcerated when he was a child. Aaron was a child who was deprived of physical affection from his parents, not only due to the choices they made but by the judgements of our society that cast him out from their arms when he needed it most.

The concept of our relationship to the soldiers who crucified Jesus on the cross is one that takes time to develop and truly comprehend as a Christian. Although, my comprehension and understanding has deepened, I sense that there is still great learning for me to do as to what my role was in the crucifixion of our precious Lord. Yet somehow when I look at Aaron's life, it's easy to see that the suffering he has endured is not just due to the consequences of poor choices on the part of his parents and poor choices of his own, but also due to harsh, cruel and unjust judgements on the part of our society as a whole. Did I hold the nail of crucifixion when I turned my eyes from imprisonment and said I didn't care because they made their choice? Did I deliver a scourging blow to our Lord's back when I turned my back on the child who longed for the parent to hold him during the long years of incarceration? And wasn't it true that I spat jeering words in the face of Christ when I mumbled profanities at the evening news of a mug shot of a man who was merely accused, whom I had already deemed guilty?

Those who have ears ought to hear, those who have eyes ought to see and those who have hearts ought to love.

Once your eyes are open to the truth, you cannot deny it, to do so is to be dishonest to yourself. We see in Acts 9 Saul's eyes temporarily blinded as he undeniably encounters Jesus. Taken from Acts 9:3–9 on his journey, as he was nearing Damascus, a light from the sky suddenly flashed around him. He fell to the ground and heard a voice saying to him, "Saul, Saul, why are you persecuting me?" He said, "Who are you, sir?" The reply came, "I am Jesus, who you are persecuting. Now get up and go into the city and you will be told what you must do." The men who were traveling with him stood speechless, for they heard the voice but could see no one. Saul got up from the ground, but when he opened his eyes he could see nothing, so they led him by the hand and brought him to Damascus. For three days he was unable to see, and he neither ate nor drank. When we encounter the living God it stops us in our tracks: it is undeniable, it is life changing! Saul wisely sat in silence waiting for God for three days. How often do we sit in silence, turning off the temptations of the world and awaiting God's directions?

I venture to say, perhaps we have never truly done this. Perhaps we have done it on some mountaintop retreat experience. Over and over we see example after example in the Bible of people, who are undoubtedly holier than we are, sitting in silence awaiting God. We see John the Baptist fasting and praying, awaiting, and listening. Later we see Jesus fast for forty days in the desert in preparation for the will of the Father. If Jesus needed to go alone to the desert and fast for forty days, how long must we rid ourselves of the things of the world to hear the will of the Father? Jesus came to teach us and to be our example. Just as we pray the Our Father as he taught us, we should fast and go off to pray as he did. We must arm ourselves with true love, which comes from God and multiplies with prayer and fasting.

CHAPTER 9

THE VALUE OF SUFFERING

We oftentimes see human suffering and think there's nothing we can do. How can I help? What difference could I make?

So what value is there in us witnessing human suffering if we cannot fix it? Does our presence really make a difference for the one who is suffering or are we just a presence reminding them of what they do not have? However, when we take the time to enter into suffering with another human being and walk the walk with them, we realize that we are more alike than we are different. We help them carry the burden and the burden then feels lighter to them. How do I know this, you may wonder? I know this because of my own experience of suffering and the value of another person willing to be a listening ear, willing to sit with me in a doctor's office, willing to cut me some slack when I really didn't deserve it because my attitude was bad.

When my father died I was nineteen years old and learned a valuable lesson, a lesson that many don't learn until later in life, if ever: the value of going to funerals. So often people make excuses to not attend funerals. We say things like, "that's just not my thing." Yet the funeral is not meant for the dead, but for the living. The funeral is to walk the walk with those who now must go on without that vital person in their life. By attending a funeral, you take the hand of the one left behind and say, "I'm here, I'm with you, I see your pain, I feel your pain with you, I acknowledge your pain." Mourners at the funeral give validity to the pain of those closest to the one who has passed.

When we pray, "God break our hearts for what breaks yours," we need to be ready for our hearts to be broken, because we are given eyes to see what breaks God's heart. This will inevitably lead to suffering, emotional suffering, on our part. Yet it allows us to see who God chooses us to administer to and who God calls us to walk with. All of our burdens are lighter when we have someone else with us in our struggle, and at the same time our struggles seem so much heavier when we feel alone. There have been many times when I knew there was just one friend who understood my position and that gave me a tremendous strength. There also have been times when I found myself mentally scrolling through my contacts in my mind wondering whom I could possibly call to share my struggle and heartache with. How lonely it felt when there was no one I could come up with. God calls us to share in the suffering of the cross. We must trust that he will give us the courage and strength to endure that suffering and to remember that it is truly worth it. The fruits of our labor can later be witnessed in the friendships we build and the revelations that we receive when meeting incredible people that we would otherwise not have known. This is certainly true of countless friends I have been blessed with, and of course Aaron is one of them.

So as Aaron told me his story, I could not help but ask this peaceful, gentle soul, why would God put you, when He is aware of your innocence, here for twenty-four years to suffer? Don't we often say of those imprisoned, "what a waste"? In such statements we are referring to a life that could have been, but was abandoned due to bad choices. Maybe we are even referring to a "waste" of taxpayer dollars to house and feed those we deem worthless, useless, dare I say, scum. These are words that make me cringe now that I know Aaron and now that I have made multiple trips to the prison and seen the countless others hidden away from the rest of us, hidden from relevancy.

Aaron writes, "The imprisoned, a forgotten population. Some believers are imprisoned for the chastisement of the Father to cause us to repent and turn to him and some innocent for God's glory to be shown. However, we who possess the Holy Bible and knowledge of it, can go to just about any chapter or book and find a prophet, holy man of God, speaking in tongues perhaps, or proclaiming the truth of God. We see these individuals experiencing some type of hardship, including imprisonment. We find them isolated in a wilderness of persecution, a host of issues that our Father has allowed. Why? Why does our Father allow this persecution, this isolation, this chastisement?"

Aaron seems to lovingly accept from God his current situation, trusting that God will provide, and rescue him from his suffering in God's appointed time, which Aaron always refers to as God's perfect time. It is impossible for me not to be drawn to and awed by that level of trust in God. It makes me ashamed of the repeated times I asked God for yet another sign after having received multiple signs that should have been clear to me. Then there were the times that I clearly understood the will of God and chose my own plan just because it seemed easier, more desirable or more acceptable to the world. I remember Aaron commenting with his easy smile that he ended up thanking God for being in prison, for the relationship that he developed that he would not have if he had not been imprisoned: his relationship with our living God. Jesus tells us, "my yoke is easy and my burden is light" (Mat. 11:30).

Often our lives seem so complicated and so messy. We feel confused and unhappy and we don't know which way to turn. We feel as though we are drowning and there is no one willing or able to throw us a lifeline. We all experience that from time to time: what a lonely, desolate place that is for our soul to struggle in. One morning as I drove my girls to school my phone repeatedly peeped with incoming text messages. My daughter asked me if I was on a group text, wondering why my phone had notified me repeatedly. I explained it was my friend Amy, who I had met briefly while shopping, and we had formed a fast friendship which had blossomed into emotional and spiritual support for one another several times a week via text messages and snap chatting. Surprised, my daughter said, "Do you two text every day?" Suddenly God had presented me with a golden opportunity to speak to my middle school daughters about true friendship. I explained that one could recognize a true friend when the relationship came easy and without chaos. My daughter quickly proclaimed, "The Devil makes things complicated, if it's complicated you know it's the Devil." So true. Sure, our heavenly Father may call us to something hard and challenging, but it is not complicated. God is clear but games of deception are always from the Devil.

To be imprisoned for thirteen years for a filthy crime he was innocent of was very challenging for Aaron, but it was not complicated. He was in a hard situation indeed, but so many obstacles had been removed to make way for a deep relationship with the Father. As I visited Aaron one sunny afternoon he easily told me, "Really, this is the greatest experience of my life." Even after knowing him for nearly a year, this statement still shocked me. Surely it's one thing to find the silver lining, but to have genuine joy while in an oppressive situation, that can only come from God. I asked Aaron to explain this further, and he explained that it's been great due to his relationship with God and all that has been given to him.

We live in a society where we strive to limit suffering. We sweep in and "save" our children from the harshness of the world, even to a fault. We soften the blow when delivering negative feedback. We are taught to give two compliments for each "opportunity" for improvement, better known as weaknesses. So what good can possibly come from suffering? Isn't there an easier way to achieve the same outcome? Aaron is one example of how suffering has brought him into relationship with God and molded him into a person that not only knows the love of God but radiates it. Therefore, Aaron's suffering has not only been fruitful for him but also for all those he comes into contact with. Perhaps the value of our suffering is not just to bring ourselves closer to Christ but perhaps our suffering is a catalyst for someone else to deepen their relationship with Christ through our example. Perhaps when someone else sees us endure suffering with grace it gives them conviction to question what they are witnessing and dig deeper to seek a deeper relationship with God themselves. When situations get particularly difficult, Aaron often asks, "Why not me?" This is in direct contrast to the typical human response of "Why me?"

My life and the life of my family changed drastically after meeting Aaron. I am not sure if I can pinpoint if it was his example, or his prayers or my own eyes opened to a reality I had not encountered before. Likely it was due to all of these factors. In one of Aaron's first correspondences to me, he told me he was fasting for my family and me. Fasting was nearly extinguished from most circles I traveled in. A few years back my husband had been counseled by a Christian friend to fast in search of answers to questions. Pat had taken the friend's advice and certainly it worked. He felt his questions were answered. Then there was the communal fasting each Lent, from no meat on Fridays to no eating in between meals, in addition to the no meat on Ash Wednesday and Good Friday. But I had to be honest, it didn't seem too depriving to attend the local fish fry each Friday. It certainly was easy to convince myself that to fast at the level of John the Baptist and Jesus in the desert was something I was not holy enough for. Wasn't it good enough for me to fast from sweets? (Plus that made fitting into the summer swim suit, which was just around the corner, a little easier). So in retrospect, it was really about… ME…not so much God. Fasting in prison, where there was no one to notice, where deprivation was in surplus, now that was about God! Aaron's fasting was about repenting for sins, his and when he fasted for me, my sins. Whoa! That was more than I was even willing to do to save my own soul, which led me to conclude that this relationship that Aaron had with God was so good that he would choose to deprive himself in an already deprived environment. Yet it was even better than that: Aaron's relationship with God was so good that he was willing to fast for someone else, someone that he really didn't know.

God's love transforms us from self-centered to Christ-centered. When we know the love of God, we want everyone we encounter to know the same love. "Everyone" includes even those who are hurtful and spiteful to us and our loved ones. Now, that is intense love: a love that penetrates hate and resentment, a love that heals and makes whole.

The more I got to know Aaron, the more I hungered to know God at the level he did. I wanted to read scripture, and even though I was notorious for lingering in bed each morning until the last possible minute, I was willing to get up earlier to spend time with God before I started the rest of my day. As I observed my friend rolling with the life he had been given, choosing joy and worshiping God in his suffering, I began to trust more and have less anxiety. When my daughters struggled, I could rest in the reassurance that God had my back. I didn't have to jump to the "what ifs?" and struggle to make a plan B. I learned through Aaron's example that I could wait patiently on God, even if that meant thirteen years, and still live in the peace and love of God.

I know I have wondered amidst suffering if I can be of value and service during such a weak personal time. While you will be amazed and awed by this story of Aaron, a Black man and his unlikely friendship with two white supremacists while in prison, it illuminates our ability to make a difference and be used by the hand of God, even amidst suffering.

We never know what domino effect may take place following our actions. For me I am most challenged to show the love of Christ to those who express hate. I know what God calls me to, but carrying that out I often feel like I don't even know where to begin. When Aaron wrote me he forgave slave owners and those who were responsible for his incarceration, it was hard to wrap my brain around as to how he could come to that place.

In October of 2016, Jodi Picoult released her book *small, great things.* In this book she courageously addresses white supremacy, institutional racism, and white privilege and touches on mass incarceration. While these are undoubtedly heavy topics to weave into her novel, her characters reach out to readers and gently expose each point of view with great finesse. She moves the characters, as well as the reader, to look at opposing viewpoints, all while emphasizing the common ground we share as those who travel this earth through the human experience.

In the spring of 2017 a friend recommended I read the book *small, great things* and after finishing it I passed it along to Aaron. I was eager for him to read it as I wanted his thoughts on the book. As Aaron finished reading *small, great things*, he became acquainted with another man who was incarcerated who happened to be a white supremacist. A Black man and a white supremacist in close quarters sounds like a recipe for disaster, and yet the unexpected outcome would amaze even me. Aaron ended up becoming friends not just with the man he was sharing a space with, but also this man's friend. Because Aaron treated this man with respect and kindness, in the period of a few short weeks he was able to share not just the book *small, great things* with these self-proclaimed white supremacists, but more importantly, Aaron was able to share the love of God. In the end, Aaron would pray over these men and they went on to share the book with other friends. Now, that's how you show God's love to another! That's how you change the world one friend at a time!

If two men in a hostile, oppressive environment can show kindness, respect and ultimately, God's love, then certainly the rest of us can do that as well. This is exactly how we need to approach the race problem in America. We can make a great impact one person at a time, but we must speak up. None of us can afford to remain silent on this issue. Dialogue has the capacity to interject new ideas, and when delivered with respect and love, can help facilitate the reception of the message.

Humiliation is far greater suffering than the most intense physical suffering. I believe it was this innate understanding that made me hesitant to ask Aaron about the humiliation he endured as a result of his incarceration and accusation of a crime he did not commit. It was one thing to see my friend economically and socially outcast, which is humiliation in itself. However, to hear those words from his experience seemed unbearable. Asking him to share on this level seemed to risk stripping him of more dignity than had already been taken. Then, I looked to the cross: was that not the ultimate stripping of dignity? How could our all-powerful, almighty God have quietly and willingly suffered at that level for us, an ungrateful hostile group of repeat offenders, who showed little hope for the prospect of rehabilitation?

To enter into a relationship with the living God implodes rehabilitation. We are at such a desperate level it requires transformation. Transformation is so much more than rehabilitation. Rehabilitation takes weeks to months: it is about restoring what was previously intact. Transformation, on the other hand, is a complete rebuilding of something that was useless and making it functional and useable. Transformation takes years…a lifetime.

Oh Lord, humility is your presentation but glory is your reality.

Understanding the value of human suffering takes spiritual eyes. When we ask, we will receive, so let us courageously ask the Holy Spirit to reveal to us the next time we encounter human suffering to not harden our hearts but rather to open them up to the unfathomable wisdom and understanding of our Creator.

Aaron writes, "Do not miss the opportunity to draw close to the Almighty." That is a strong warning and message of encouragement from someone who has walked the road of suffering for dare I say nearly, if not completely, his entire life.

CHAPTER 10

WE ARE CALLED.
WILL WE ANSWER?

"I, a prisoner for the Lord, urge you to live
in a manner worthy of the call you have
received, with all humility and gentleness,
with patience, bearing with one another
through love, striving to preserve the unity
of the Spirit through the bond of peace."
—Ephesians 4:1–5.

Jesus tells us in Matthew 25:31–46:

When the Son of Man comes in his glory
and all the angels with him, he will sit upon his
glorious throne, and all the nations will be assem-
bled before him. And he will separate them one
from another, as a shepherd separates the sheep
from the goats. He will place the sheep on his
right and the goats on his left. Then the king
will say to those on his right, 'Come, you who
are blessed by my Father. Inherit the kingdom
prepared for you from the foundation of the
world. For I was hungry and you gave me food,

I was thirsty and you gave me drink, a stranger and you welcomed me, naked and you clothed me, ill and you cared for me, in prison and you visited me.' Then the righteous will answer him and say, 'Lord, when did we see you hungry and feed you, or thirsty and give you drink? When did we see you a stranger and welcome you, or naked and clothed you? When did we see you ill or in prison, and visit you?' And the king will say to them in reply, 'Amen, I say to you, whatever you did for one of these least brothers of mine, you did for me.' Then, he will say to those on his left, 'Depart from me, you accursed, into the eternal fire prepared for the Devil and his angels. For I was hungry and you gave me no food, I was thirsty and you gave me no drink, a stranger and you gave me no welcome, naked and you gave me no clothing, ill and in prison and you did not care for me.' Then they will answer and say, 'Lord, when did we see you hungry or thirsty or a stranger or naked or ill or in prison, and not minister to your needs?' He will answer them, 'Amen, I say to you, whatever you did not do for one of these least ones, you did not do for me.' And these will go off to eternal punishment, but the righteous to eternal life."

Years earlier, Aaron had shared this scripture with an individual he had gone to high school with, after the individual had written Aaron a few times and made a visit to clear his conscience. This man was a professed Christian. Aaron did not hear from this man again. Later Aaron was informed that this very man had moved out of state to pursue a pastoral position! How do we share the love of Jesus when we cannot recognize it within us? The struggle remains in leadership today, as it was in Jesus' time on earth. Like the Pharisees, there are leaders today professing to be holy men and women of God who know about Jesus, but do not have a personal relationship with Jesus. They work tirelessly to "make people see." When a person truly knows God and has a relationship with Jesus, the love of the Father flows freely, effortlessly.

A man claiming to be of God, but not acting as such, is no surprise. This has been a sin dating back to biblical times. The point of interest in this story is Aaron's response. Aaron writes me that from the depths of his soul, he prays for God's blessing on this individual who has abandoned him in his hour of need. This reminds me of the shocking greeting Jesus has for his apostles after the resurrection: "Peace be with you." Only a soul in unity with the living God can extend a greeting of peace to friends who have abandoned you in your hour of need. In that simple greeting, Jesus conveys his love and forgiveness for his friends. That is the God we serve! A GOD who cares about our feelings and about us, no matter what we have done. And that is the very God who has stood by Aaron in what he calls his time in the "wilderness."

It is from that very vantage point of being abandoned and living on the fringes that great clarity of actions can best be observed. Aaron explains, "Our Lord and Savior was himself imprisoned. From this prison cell we see everyone's actions clearly, we do not forget the mercy that's shown, the love that is suffocated, but most importantly we pay close attention to professed believers who possess the Holy Bible, and what their actions are."

It was this very passage from Matthew chapter 25 that had beckoned to me for years. I had been blessed to meet the face of Jesus in those I interacted with daily, in the face of the sick who were so very often hungry and thirsty and helpless. However, I felt I had not had an opportunity to be the face of Jesus to the imprisoned. I began to pray that God would allow me to be his hands and feet to the imprisoned. God's gifts always exceed our expectation. I went to the prison to meet Aaron and be Jesus to him, but the abundant gift that God had for me in Aaron exceeded what I had to offer to Aaron. Why was I surprised that was how God worked? God called me and then blessed me one hundred times over.

CHAPTER 11

Trusting in the Power of God to Bring Us Out of Prison

One can be reminded how God works when looking at the story of Moses and how God used him in his human weakness to do great things. Moses was born into a dicey situation: there was a decree that all Hebrew boys were to be murdered at birth. Moses' mother acted quickly and cleverly to make an adoption plan for her son. Moses grows up observing his very people instead of living beside them; he enjoys privileges that no Israelite slave could dream of. Yet Moses realizes who he is: an Israelite. When he witnesses mistreatment of a fellow Israelite, he lashes out, rebelling against the system by killing the Egyptian. In a panic, Moses runs to save his own life. It is at this very point that God speaks to this murderer on the run, who undoubtedly was confused by his own identity, growing up outside of his own people. We can see his wavering self-esteem and we hear him complain to God about his lack of eloquent speech. Of course, God already knows all this of Moses and he chooses him anyway. Why? God saw in Moses a humble prophet who would listen attentively and do miracles in the name of God to free the people of Israel. Only God can do this! Why, we must ask ourselves, do we waver in trusting God to do the same in our lives? Why wouldn't God want our hearts' deepest, purest desires to come to be? Is it not He who planted those very desires?

These were the very questions that God spoke to me as Aaron demanded I trust God more. "More" was actually a really nice way to put it. I was under the illusion that I *was* trusting God, but my own self-doubt perpetuated by "realism" kept me imprisoned from the freedom of living in the security and love of God. In my mind I would think, "I know God could heal me, but will He choose to do that?" This put me into an untrusting mindset. I was asking for God to help, but then making a plan B. In everything we must trust God to be our plan A, and let go of the idea of plan B. Imagine how much time we have wrapped up in making plan B, when we could be using that time to live with love and to praise our God. We are free, but we must accept it! God's gifts have already been given, it's time we be unleashed from the bondage of our fear and self-doubt. Each and every time we see Jesus healing in the New Testament, the key ingredient is faith. In order for God to provide healing in our lives to transform us and make us anew in whatever capacity we need and request, faith must be present.

So many of us wallow in our own self-imposed prisons: prisons of shame, guilt and self-doubt. It is necessary for us to turn our attention to those factors which limit us from becoming our best self, a child of God. We need to take it one step further than just the realization that we are a child of God. It sounds really nice, but what does that really mean? Doesn't that mean that we should be living free like Aaron? The thing about prison is this: you can't free yourself, you can't let yourself out. To be imprisoned means that you are trapped inside, without a way out. Just as it is completely impossible for Aaron to walk out of prison without the door being unlocked, it is completely impossible for you and me to set ourselves free from our shame, guilt and self-doubt. Simply put, you and I need God. In growing in my relationship with our Father, I realized that I was erroneously professing that I was trusting God, but really I was waiting to see what would happen, hoping for the best but not believing it. There is a difference between trusting God and testing God. This seems like an obvious statement, however, I realized that what

I believed to be trust was really testing God. In my mind I was praying, "God could you please do this? I know you could if you choose," and then waiting to see if God chose to. True trust and faith in God meant trusting that God would do what was best for me and stay by my side at all times. My job was to wait patiently for his perfect time, knowing that he heard my prayer and he sought my best interest.

For me, my self-imposed prison was fear. Fear controlled my decisions. It was so comfortable to make the safe choice. There were so many fears: fear of failure, of course; fear of the unknown; fear of rejection; fear of standing out and not blending in; fear of desired expectations not being met. What if people didn't agree with me or turned against me? What if the people I love the most, my children, my husband, my family, my close friends didn't agree with me? How might they react? It was so easy for me to stay in line and be part of the status quo because when my mind wandered to the possibilities, fear jerked me back to the false illusion that the fear itself had created. Fear had a powerful grip on me. It demanded my constant attention. I could not make a decision without "consulting" fear, answering the questions of what others would say or think. I was busy attending to the demands of what if something went wrong. Fear imprisoned me to the point of limiting me from considering the possibilities. What if I took a risk, made a move outside of the accepted and known common practice and what if that risk turned out to be the greatest joy and success of my life?

God desires peace for us. Anxiety, I have learned, comes only from the Devil. Praise be to God, He pursues us! People will comment that "they found Jesus." While I understand the turning point in one's life when Jesus enters in, I think it is Jesus who finds us. We are the lost sheep whom he has pursued. He calls our name, over and over and over again, and He will continue to pursue us tirelessly, because He created us and He loves us. He desires us, which was the only reason he became God incarnate, the only reason for the cross.

In my work as a therapist, a great challenge is to work with the patient who has a fear of falling. It is the very fear of falling that increases the risk of falling. It is the patient who has accepted that falling is just part of the equation of possibility who can truly live freely with whatever the disability is. On the contrary, some patients are crippled by the fear of falling to the point of detriment to their health. This is the most difficult type of patient to have, because when it comes time to stand, even with the support of two, three, or even four therapists, it can be impossible. Sometimes the patient would use all the physical strength available to push back instead of forward when it came time to stand. The coaching of the therapist was to no avail. When the therapist would try a soothing, understanding voice with simple directions, fear would entangle all reasoning. If the therapist would give a firm directive command, the patient would resist and retreat to fear.

Just as God reaches for us, there comes a point when we need to take His hand and trust. We must do this even when we can't see where He is leading us, even when our brains cannot fathom the outcome, even when no solution seems feasible. When we fall, we have to be willing to try to get up. This is our choice, our God-given free will. We can choose to trust God or die with our fear. As I write these words, it seems so simple and yet for me, as for so many, it is incredibly difficult. The obvious answer is to trust God, to follow His direction and get up. YET when you are down, it can be so overwhelmingly confusing and crippling. The answer to fear is faith: a blind trust that God is who He says He is. God is still in the business of healing the crippled and making the blind see. Just as it was faith that healed in the gospel, so it remains today.

It was a beautiful day, a perfect August day for a wedding. In fact it was the day of Aaron's sister, Tierra's, wedding. If there was one person who most understood Aaron's difficult childhood, it was undoubtedly Tierra. Tierra was just eleven months younger than Aaron; she often referred to him as her twin. Tierra was the only family member who had stood by his side consistently since his imprisonment. Just as Tierra had been a support to Aaron, he had been to her as well. So on this beautiful day in August as she walked down the aisle, Tierra would carry the loss of her brother's presence in her heart. At the same time, while Aaron's family would celebrate and enjoy each other's company, he would remain isolated and alone. Sometimes it is very difficult to trust in God's providence when he allows his children to suffer at such a deep level. While my heart ached for both of them on this beautiful day, Aaron later gently corrected me that "God has allowed me to experience this wilderness with Him being the focal point, guiding me through the darkness."

Yet God was ever working. Aaron's son, who was now eighteen, would bravely come to the wedding to celebrate with many family members he was meeting for the first time. Aaron's son had just graduated high school and was on his way to college. While his father was not there to protect him, God had heard the prayers of his father from prison and blessed and carried Aaron's son—carried him to a place of opportunity and protected him from the challenges Aaron himself had faced. God had not abandoned Aaron, nor his son, their stories had His glory written all over them.

Undoubtedly, a trying time for every parent is a child's teen years. We live in an age where parents often parent out of the fear of what if my child gets involved with this or that. Having teenagers in the world where you are not able to help guide them on a day-to-day basis is petrifying for most. Aaron speaks of parenting from prison: "I'm speaking from a teaching, paying attention and take no one you love for granted position. The challenges of being here in prison, the wilderness, as your children grow into young adults, encountering everyday teen drama that you can't on demand guide them through, makes you pray harder and trust God more, because things are simply out of your hands and reach. Every child deserves a loving father and mother, no one should be shortchanged from that. After all no child asked to come here, so it does take a village to raise a child; that village is us, America. Yes. Jesus, reminded us to love our neighbors as we love ourselves."

We must remember and give thanks that God does not think, love or act like us. His gifts are unimaginably endless. Just when we think we understand, we comprehend, that is the very point when God reveals one more part of who He is and our love for our Father grows even more. When we show just one baby step of trust, we see God's wisdom and love revealed to us, and with each step the view becomes clearer and clearer.

CHAPTER 12

GOD MEETS US
WHERE WE ARE

God meets us where we are; His love penetrates all barriers whether that be our physical situation of poverty or illness, drug addiction or emotional walls we build to preserve our persona, ego, or self-image. God is greater, bigger and unimaginably expansive. Sometimes we secure ourselves behind walls that protect what is most vulnerable: our hearts and egos, but remember, He who made us has the one true key to each of our hearts. Our souls were made by Him and for Him. This is so very unimaginable at times, most especially when we are locked in the dungeon of our own despair. However the flicker of hope we have deep within lights up at the tiniest spark of belief that our situation can improve, at the idea that we can survive whatever dungeon we are in. THAT is God! Most challenging to our egos is to allow that tiniest flicker to ignite and suddenly God is remodeling our hearts. Once we get a taste of His peace our souls cannot be satisfied by anything else.

It was December 25, 2011, the blanket of the night sky seemed to tuck us in, all was calm and quiet. I lay in the hospital bed gazing out the window, lying as still as possible, grateful for no immediate need to move. While it was true that my three young daughters ages three, five, and six were at home with my husband and I was not there with them on this pinnacle of family days, the Peace of

Almighty God filled my soul. My iPod, set to the Christian radio station, played "Winter Snow" by Audrey Assad, followed by the song "Your Grace is Enough." My soul sang out and soon my voice followed. Now that my body was physically still, halted in time, my soul had the freedom to run: to run into the arms of Jesus.

So on Christmas night, God met me where I was, in a hospital bed, alone, much like how he met the humble shepherds over two thousand years ago. It was not a Rockefeller Christmas, but it was perhaps the best Christmas I've ever had. There simply was nothing to tend to, because I couldn't. So I let go, accepted God's merciful invitation and just simply existed with my God. Simple, so very simple, and yet it had taken me so long to get there. I didn't need the perfect feast, or tree or gift or even church service to have a blessed Christmas; I needed Jesus. The same Jesus who had been given over two thousand years earlier. Why had it taken so long to realize that?

Audrey Assad sang "you came like a winter snow, you were quiet, you were soft and slow." When our lives are noisy and chaotic we miss Him, because He is a gentle God: slow to anger, rich in kindness. He is the God of humility and peace. Our boisterous ways, our flashy ways are not His ways. If we are looking to find God, we must go where He is. He can be found where He was found two-thousand years ago, living among the outcasts, the undesirables, those on the fringes of society.

God's ways are not our ways. They never were and they still are not. God is the same yesterday, today and tomorrow.

God met Aaron crushed in spirit in a county jail cell. The voice of the detectives echoed in Aaron's head, "You are going to the county jail." The weight of the statement pulled him to his knees in the interrogation room. While Aaron maintained his innocence of the crime he was accused of, in his heart he held the weight of the sinful life he had been living. How could his life have come to this? He did all he knew to do, from the depths of his soul he cried out to Jesus, a Jesus, he didn't really know, a Jesus whose name he had heard repeatedly roll off the sweet lips of his dear Madea. After all he had done, after who he had become, would this Jesus be there in his hour of need as Madea had repeatedly taught him?

The redeeming answer for Aaron, as it is for all of us, was ABSOLUTELY God would be there. Aaron would come to learn and know Jesus, to know that Jesus was the only one he could ever really count on, and the only one he would ever really need.

As the cell door clanged shut, the reality of his situation settled in. There was no longer a way to escape, physically or mentally. Aaron was assigned to a single men's cell. He describes, "I was boxed in with me, myself and these burdens of sin. I realized I couldn't go where I believed I was heading (at twenty-one years of age)." Aaron met God where so many do, when there is nothing else, when there is no one else. He sat alone, isolated, pleading and crying profusely to God, asking to be forgiven for all his sins, things he had seen and things he had done. Completely exposed to God in his most hopeless and broken state, God's glory illuminated that dark day. This would be the first day, yet not the last, that our Lord would appear to Aaron. In this place of despair, peace, joy and love washed over Aaron as he looked through the double glass door from the cell to see the precious face of Jesus. Aaron was not alone to carry the burden of his sin; he was forgiven! In the days to come, his faith would continue to grow, spreading like wildfire. As he studied the Bible with two other inmates, Jesus would appear again, this time the face of the suffering Christ. A crown of thorns encircled his head, blood ran down his suffering face. Aaron describes that he had a full beard and long hair, his eyes were wide-open, peering into Aaron's soul.

If you were to meet Aaron, you would first notice his sense of peace and freedom. This is a shock, given his current location! And if you were to ask Aaron about the source of that peace and freedom, the smile would grow on his face and his eyes would grow even brighter and he would proudly boast of the love of God! Without a hint of doubt, Aaron would begin to tell you about the grace that has been bestowed upon him in prison, the blessing to know Almighty God. He is a living breathing miracle, a work of Almighty God. As verification of authenticity is Aaron's pure love for God, which is observed in his forgiveness of the multitude of people from his mother and father, to his accuser, to failed attorneys. Love is the key to freedom; it is love that reigns and that has given Aaron peace. When you have that much love, you have to share it because that is the very essence of love. It is true that God is love and just as God cannot be contained, nor can love, it must be shared. The God who believed that Aaron could change, the God who pursued Aaron, is the same God who believes in you and me and pursues us with his endless, infinite love.

CHAPTER 13

HOW PRISON CHANGED ME

We never know who our teachers are going to be. We only need to be humble enough to accept them.

The first time I visited Aaron was my first time in a prison. It was impossible not to notice the racially skewed population of incarcerated individuals. On only my second visit, the prison staff remembered me. Why? Because I was not the norm when it came to the profile of a visitor. As a white middle-class, middle-aged woman, I stood out like a sore thumb.

After I had been going to visit Aaron on a monthly basis for eight months, something unusual began to happen. When I entered the first door, the guard at the check-in desk recognized me by name. If you have not been to visit someone in prison, you may be inclined to think this was to be expected or was not that big of a deal. In all my time going to visit Aaron never have I noticed even one other visitor who was identifiable by name, as well as by the inmate whom the person was visiting. Before I would even get to check in, the guard would pick up the phone, call Aaron's cell block, and announce that there was a visit for Aaron. It was November of 2016. The guard released the first of a series of doors for me to go through to let me into the prison. As I opened the door, I thought I heard, "Naderman." Surprised and a little fearful, I tried to rationalize in my mind, no it couldn't be. Sometimes I would see families that looked familiar to me, families that had been on visits on days I had been to visit previously. Never had I noticed that the guards were familiar enough with these visitors that they remembered their names and the names of the inmates that were being visited. I sat in the waiting room, my heart pounding, hands shaking as my mind raced to what the "pat-down" process may entail now that I was "identified." Thankfully, to this day I have been treated with respect and the process has remained the same. Nevertheless, I remain mindful that at any time, something may change.

Tierra, Aaron's sister was instrumental in arranging for Aaron's two children to meet each other and to encourage their relationship with their father. After all they were five and one at the time of his incarceration. How many of our friends, neighbors and coworkers quietly carry this cross of incarcerated loved ones, silently alone? I think of all the times I heard or made casual, thoughtless remarks regarding the prison population: "They're animals," "they deserve it," "I can't believe my tax dollars go for them to watch cable TV," "I don't care, they could take the key and throw it away for all I care!" OUCH, those words stung now; those words were no longer funny or accepted. They hurt.

The magnitude of how widespread mass incarceration is in the Black community became very apparent to me one afternoon. I was working on writing this book and wanted to get Tierra's perspective on the experience of visiting her brother in prison. I began texting with Tierra, or so I thought. It turns out I was texting with another Tierra in my contact list. I had met this other Tierra while working on a project with the non-profit, Moms for Tomorrow. Moms for Tomorrow, Inc. is a grassroots non-profit started by six moms with the mission of helping mothers and children in need. After a lengthy text, I realized that this was not Tierra, Aaron's sister. We laughed a little about the mix-up, but for me it opened my eyes to mass incarceration even more. To be Black in America meant knowing someone in prison. Tierra describes the visits to prison as full of love, all smiles even when there are disagreements. Regarding visits in which she had to deliver bad news like the death of a loved one, she says, "its heart crushing, like you are the judge that sentenced your loved one." For Tierra, visiting a loved one in prison was not just about companionship for him, but she often had to follow up after the visit to pass along communication from other inmates who lacked phone access. Some inmates lose phone privileges and others lack the resources to finance phone calls.

It is important to realize that Tierra and I had not had contact for over a year. She was in my contacts, but we had little to no contact after the project was completed. Yet when I texted her about her experience of visiting prison, she was quick to honestly respond. Due to our work on the project a year ago, there was a sense of trust between us, yet nonetheless, she had never revealed to me that she had family and friends who were incarcerated. Incarceration among those who were poor was so common that I didn't even have to ask her if she had ever been to visit a loved one in prison; it was a given in her experience.

The other families and friends on visiting days always caught my attention. My heart always broke when I heard a visitor announce that their relationship to the inmate was "mother" or "father." How helpless and devastating it must be to visit your son or daughter in prison. Seeing the children of the inmates was also heartbreaking. There are rules of physical contact: a brief hug and kiss are permitted at the beginning and end of the visit. Children are never allowed to sit on the lap of the inmate. How much love and security does a child feel when they are held by a parent? Would the tenderness of holding a child calm the soul of the stressed out, rejected inmate? Would sitting on daddy's lap for an hour once a month help to settle the angry, confused child who felt rejected? Why is a child punished for the sins of the parent? Does the deprivation of holding your child promote rehabilitation? I recall the joy that would spread across my grandfather's face when I would bring my babies to visit him in the nursing home. One of my very favorite photographs is my grandfather holding my daughter, who was nine months at the time. The joy on his face radiates out of the photo to touch the heart of the onlooker. Imagine what that joy felt like on the inside!

As impossible as it was for me to go unnoticed, it was even more impossible for me to not notice the immense and holy presence of God within the wall of this prison. In an age where we look at our phones, mumble responses and make minimal eye contact, here sat a room full of people engaging in pure and real conversations without the distraction of technology, without a prestigious title to hide behind or a drink in hand to take the edge off. This was rare! Looking around the room, I could see genuine smiles, real conversations and quality time being shared. I always felt bonded to those who were entering the prison to visit on the same day as I was. We were a group of people who shared the sorrow of our loved one locked away, rejected by society. We were a group who would return to work the next day and not include this in our water cooler conversation. We were a group eager to see our loved one, and yet fearful of the state of mind we may find him in.

There was always the occasional visitor that was reprimanded; more often than not it was clothing that the visitor was wearing that was the problem. One day I was sent home to change because my shirt was deemed too low necked. This was the shirt I planned to wear when I went to work at the nursing home when I left the visit! The day that a six-year-old was told her pants were inappropriate because they had spandex in them felt like harassment. Families often drove hours to visit, so at 8:00 a.m. on a Saturday morning it was understandable that this little girl was groggy. She likely had just woken up from a long car ride. As her grandmother brushed her hair each strand clung to the brush with the static that plagued each fine-haired child in January. I noticed this family. Clearly it was grandma and grandpa bringing the little girl to visit her daddy. The little girl was neatly dressed. She sported the ever-popular leggings that my girls wore each day to school, and I presumed they were likely a Christmas present. Just like my girls, the leggings were loose fitting on her skinny little active legs. The door opened to enter the pat-down room, this family was called forward and then informed that the six-year-old's pants were not permitted. The female guard quietly, almost ashamedly, explained that her sergeant behind the Plexiglas had noticed the pants. Grandma and Grandpa did a good job of remaining calm and asking where the nearest Target was to purchase something more appropriate. My heart pounded as my blood seemed to boil at the disgust of this middle-aged man visually examining the clothing of an innocent, groggy six-year-old here to visit her daddy. Why couldn't she just remember an uplifting day of visiting Daddy? I prayed that she would not get the message that she was dressed inappropriately at this young age. How had the sergeant gotten so far from compassion? Perhaps he was the greatest tragedy of loss in this moment.

Coming from privileged America, one might have expected to observe "ghetto," trashy, outrageous behavior that lacked class, and yet this was never my experience of other visitors. Often there were exchanges of sympathetic smiles as we waited and casual conversation to ease the tension. When someone was targeted for inappropriate clothing, there was a collective palpable feeling of empathy that hugged the air. When the vending card machine wouldn't take our cash, we exchanged bills with each other. In the pat-down room when I was asked if I was wearing underwear, it was the knowledge that I was not alone in this degrading invasion that allowed me to answer "yes" with dignity.

If Jesus is there, why aren't we? This is a critical question that every person who professes to know and love Jesus needs to ask himself. We must remember that WE SERVE a GOD who was and is humble. Almighty God was born in a barn. Almighty God uttered no cry when he was called a heretic and labeled a criminal. If we profess that our God did all this, then why do we work tirelessly to achieve our own greatness and glory? Surely this is not God's way. Scripture clearly shows us from Old Testament to New Testament not only who God is, but what God wants.

He was born poor and died a criminal. If we are not working with these two populations, we are missing the boat. We must critically ask ourselves why Jesus, the Son of the Living God, chose to be born poor and die a criminal, choosing complete humility. Those are questions that we could meditate on endlessly. They are worth our time to meditate on and God calls us to it. We will know our purpose when we meditate through these two ideas.

God's ways are not our ways and so we have tried to make God like us! We have tried to polish up God's image in order to make him fit our idea of who he should be. We use God as a punishment as we see fit to condemn those we deem unworthy. We ignore God's command to live humble lives of service. We seek power and prestige and stand on our soap box demanding that God bless us.

A critical question we need to ask ourselves is: Do we really want a GOD like us? A GOD who measures achievement by dollars in the bank? A GOD who says "she'll never change"? How approachable would God be if he put his glory before his humility? But rather, with our God, it is his very humble nature that his great glory shines through. God wants us. He wants our hearts. It is because we can trust God to forgive that we are able to approach him in humility, beg his endless mercy, seek his love and call him friend.

CHAPTER 14

CHANGING ONE
STEP AT A TIME

Our beginning does not determine our end! Praise be to God!
Aaron's story is really the timeless story of God working out of our
weakness to create a masterpiece.

We can all easily agree that a drug dealer is a bad dude, but what
if that drug dealer is a ten-year-old boy? At this point, it is a game-
changer. When I dug deeper to understand that Aaron was being
groomed for life in the gang even before he had entered school, it
became a story of epic tragedy. How can we cast blame on a child?
What responsibility does our society have? As the white privileged
majority, we cannot dust off our hands and shake our heads saying it
is a Black problem. How could the Black community ever begin to
chip away at this problem without the support of the community as
a whole? Are we expecting overburdened mothers to solve this? The
Black man has been removed from the relevant on so many levels
in our society. Perhaps we begin with acknowledging the situation
and agree that we will begin with seeing the tragedy from a different
vantage point. Perhaps we begin with a commitment to refuse to
blame. The refusal of blame, alone, will convict us to action and
compassion.

The lack of role models for Black males, for young boys, is
a result of mass incarceration. Black men are removed, and then

returned with the label of damaged and unusable. It is a label noted on each application for employment and housing. It is a label felt by each hushed voice who makes excuses for why the man is not eligible. It is a label internalized and eventually believed by each man who carries the baggage of previous incarceration.

There will always be the exception, just as Einstein is the exception to expected achievement. A parent does not look at his or her newborn baby with the expectation that he or she will be the next Einstein. The parent looks at his or her life and hopes the child will do a little better than the parent has. Therefore, a child born into a system of reduced opportunity, struggle, lack of positive role models and a societal mark of reduced expectation of what the outcome will be, is already at a disadvantage. The parents have a view which is clouded in daily struggle; society has set an expected outcome, even before that child entered the school system. In Aaron's case, his formation to fit into the societal expectation began so very early. By the time his brain reached full development, which scientists tell us is twenty-five years of age for males, he was already incarcerated. In my mind that is a crime. We have failed as a society.

Often when I went to visit Aaron, I would again be startled by the baby-faced inmates. It was the lanky frame and awkward stroll as he entered the room. It was a hint of a shadow on his upper lip that yet did not require a razor. It was these moments that I was always grateful that I had not known Aaron when he was that young man at twenty-one. I always noticed them, but couldn't look long; it was too much to bear. These young men were always visited by their parents. It was always a distressing sight and there was always at least one in the room, and unfortunately often more.

CHAPTER 15

WE ARE CALLED TO CARE: WITH ACTION

"Why do they do that?" "Why don't they, just...?" The smug face of white privilege judges from afar. The arrow of judgement sears with "I know if it were me... I would..." It is only from the position of privilege, a place of guaranteed security that they can gaze from afar and surmise. If you have begun a sentence with any of these phrases, it is time for you to admit at least to yourself that you have been guilty of racism.

It was easy for the jury to convict Aaron. Here was yet another young Black male who didn't have a job, who was caught walking the streets with a group of friends midday, dressed in dark clothes. When the all-white jury saw Aaron, they were familiar with his type. Here was a young man who had the hope of a successful life who instead chose the life of crime. That was to be expected, of course; he was from the infamous part of town. His attorney hid behind his title and image, delivering his own punishment when Aaron would not provide information he wanted. As a young twenty-one-year-old in the "justice" system for the first time, surely Aaron did not believe the threats of his attorney to "sell him down the river" if he did not provide information on his brothers' whereabouts.

It's easy for us to make excuses as to why this issue is not our issue to work to solve. Let me address a few of the common excuses:

I don't know enough about it to get involved. This statement can really be paraphrased as "I don't care enough about it to get involved." We live in the age of information. We constantly get information we desire when we desire it.

It doesn't affect me. My response to this is: YES, IT DOES!! As Christians, whether we want to accept it or not, when one part of the body of Christ is hurting, it affects the whole body. When I walk into my children's school, the injustice to the Black male is obvious in the faces of over-burdened mothers and children accustomed to going without. An all too common sight is that of the adult Black male role model being the elderly grandfather trying to fill the void or the young Black man aimlessly following the mother and small children. If my daughters' classmates are affected, then my daughters are affected. If my co-workers are affected, it impacts my work environment. What matters to one of us matters to all of us. While we can deny it, the truth and reality of it remains.

What difference can I make anyway? This question could best be answered by Aaron. What difference did it make if one person cared or not? Oftentimes it is the concern of just one individual that gives us the courage to go on and gives us hope for tomorrow. Each of us needs to feel the love of God shine through in another human being. This is why Jesus lived in a community, following common human practices like sharing a meal and going to the temple. Visiting Aaron, accepting him for who he was and being his friend, lightened his burden and gave him hope. Each time Aaron received a letter or a visit he was reminded that he was not alone; he was not forgotten; he was relevant.

Nothing is perfect, everybody has problems. True, but thankfully most of us don't have problems like Aaron. Just because we, too, carry our own crosses does not mean that we can't help others carry theirs. Isn't that what it means to be the body of Christ? Jesus didn't tell us to love one another and to love our neighbor as ourselves because it sounded nice in a utopian sort of a way, but because that is actually what he wants us to do! He also didn't instruct us to wait to love our neighbor as ourselves once we got our own lives in order. His message is to love your neighbor as yourself, especially when it is difficult.

It's not my thing. How many times have you heard someone say they don't go to funerals because they don't like them? Perhaps the better question is, how many times have you heard someone say they go to funerals because they love them? The point is, we all are required to do acts that are outside of our comfort zone. Especially as Christians, we are called to continually go outside our comfort zones and minister to those in need. No one likes messy situations, yet it is part of the human experience. We are going to all have to work together, which will inevitably involve getting our hands dirty, to fix the problems our society faces as a whole.

Allowing the mercy of God to work through us comes at a high price. Anthony Stolen puts it best when he states that, "Mercy costs us in sweat and time. Mercy demands that we listen even to the rambles of a bad or sick man." Everyone must get their hands dirty to solve the race problem in America. Everyone must put in sweat and time to solve this injustice.

There was a discomfort, really a fear, within me in going to visit Aaron that first time. I was, after all, going to visit someone I had never met before in an environment I had never been in. It was this completely unknown world to me, only vaguely familiar via movies. I was surprised on the third visit that I was still feeling discomfort. What was that, I pondered to myself? It was only when Aaron made a joke of standing up on top of the table and giving glory to God and I quickly said, "Please don't" that I had an opportunity to understand my discomfort. I thought about it in the days to follow and it became clear to me that my real concern was what the actions of the guards would be in such a circumstance. Surely it would involve wrestling to the ground and undue force. That was it! The anxiety I experienced with going to visit Aaron was a deep fear of witnessing human suffering and injustice. How many others stood back and did not get involved out of fear of witnessing human suffering and injustice that once seen you cannot erase from your memory? There would never be a time from now on that I would drive past the prison and not remember all those families sharing in the visiting room. Forever imprinted in my memory was the sea of Black men dressed in blue, a scene of skewed diversity. When we choose not to get involved, we preserve our emotional well-being. We save ourselves from the suffering of knowing another's anguish. While we preserve and save ourselves, we also deny ourselves the opportunity to be God and see God in the face of another human. As Christians we are called to so much more. We are called to live in solidarity with our neighbor. In the family of God, our neighbor is each human being who walks this earth.

It was larger than even that: the denied sunsets, the denied summer breeze, a hot cup of coffee just the way you like it, the inability to choose any and everything. After meeting Aaron it was also impossible not to be so grateful for everything in my life. That gratitude began with the circumstance I was born into: white, middle-class, Midwestern, two parents living in the same home. All of that instantly set me on a path for what society expected from me and looked forward to being achieved by me. What did our society expect from Aaron the day he was born? It seemed by studying our history, viewing our media and watching our interactions, Aaron had met the expectation. That is devastating! I don't know about you, but I cannot walk away from that level of inequity.

If you don't believe racism is a problem in America today, then ask yourself this question: Would you have a problem if you woke up tomorrow and were Black? Reflect on how your life would be different.

Galatians 6:2–5

Bear one another's burdens, and so you will fulfill the law of Christ. For if anyone thinks he is something when he is nothing, he is deluding himself. Each one must examine his own work, and then he will have reason to boast with regard to himself alone, and not with regard to someone else; for each will bear his own load.

The smug, sly schemes of racism today require our watchful eye. It is easy to breeze past the headlines and skim the photos, quickly assessing and concluding. Yet when we read into the article and look behind the clever wording, we see a different story. This was true in the case of Charles Kinsey.

"It could have been me," was the thought that ran through my mind over and over after reading the July 20, 2016 article in the Miami Herald. Charles Kinsey was on the clock, doing what he always did, putting the residents first. When a twenty-three-year-old man wandered out of the group home, Kinsey calmly went to assist him back in. When Kinsey found the resident was sitting in the middle of the street he calmly moved in beside him, as he had been taught to defuse tense situations, and build confidence. In all Kinsey's training, as with all human service professionals, he was taught to put the needs of the resident first. Mr. Kinsey was focused and calm. He was confident he could coax the man off the street and back into the group home, and until that happened it was Mr. Kinsey's job to keep the man safe. No one could have imagined that Mr. Kinsey would end up being shot by the police. Mr. Kinsey was unarmed. Mr. Kinsey lay on the ground with his hands up saying "don't shoot." So why did the officer shoot Mr. Kinsey? Mr. Kinsey was calm and articulate, but he was a Black man in America in the summer of 2016. Mr. Kinsey spent his days earning his living caring for those who could not care for themselves. I understood the ability to put your own desires aside and work for those you served. When my patients succeeded, it always made my day; it made it all worth it. Mr. Kinsey was just doing his job, putting someone else's life in a place of higher importance than his own; how familiar that was to me. What was different for me however, was my ability to be protected by the color of my skin. My actions whether at work or in other social settings were presumed innocent until proven otherwise.

As the racial divide widened in the America in the summer of 2016, I could sense a change in myself. Initially it was a fire in my stomach, an anger from the repeated injustice. But as the summer progressed, so did the bloodshed, and the anger within me began to turn to sorrow. I began to question, rather than blame. What had gone so wrong? Where and when did we begin to fail each other at this level? Our academic scores showed we were smarter. We were technologically advantaged with information right at our fingertips and yet the best we could do was to live in a society that was growing in fear and hate, quick to blame someone else. It was time that we each took responsibility and began making changes in our homes, in our workplaces and in our social circles. No longer could we sit quietly when a friend or family member made a racial slight. It was time to step out and stand up. People were being executed because of the color of their skin and people were being hunted down because of their profession. We could no longer wish it away. Change required action from all, not just from a few. We couldn't wait to join a movement. We needed to start right where we were.

It was time we stopped praying it would all just go away and start asking God what we could do to help. It was time we asked God to allow us to see each other through His eyes. It was time we prayed for the courage to speak up when comments were made. It was time we asked God to teach us how to love.

After meeting Aaron, I could no longer accept the excuse that some people were just so different than me that "we had nothing in common." The friendship between Aaron and me was proof that two people from very different backgrounds had much in common. When it came to life experiences, at a glance it seemed Aaron and I had little, if any, shared life experiences. Yet the truth was that we both had experienced love and loss: the two great teachers in life. Imagine a world in which we first looked for similarities and hyper-focused on our sameness rather than our differences. Wouldn't our hearts break with our neighbor's loss and our hearts burst with joy in our neighbor's gain? Wouldn't we all soar with success if we were surrounded by encouragement and a desire to understand? I want that for my children and for myself, but also for those I encounter because that environment can only yield peace.

Several years ago my youngest daughter developed pneumonia as a result of the H1N1 virus. She was two-years-old at the time and nearly died. After a very scary two week stay in the hospital and two surgeries, one to remove a portion of her lung that had necrosis, we were finally home, with our precious baby girl with us, all five of us together again. My doorbell rang and I opened the door to find Tom, my friend and co-worker, standing with a meat and cheese tray. As it turned out, his father-in-law had just died, and his family had received an over-abundance of food. Even though Tom was mourning the loss of his father-in-law, he had the kindness to think of my family and me and rejoice with us at our daughter's recovery. While Tom has now passed and has gone on to be with the Lord, I think of him often. His kind act to my family and me motivated me to give to others more. Jesus rejoiced with friends at the wedding feast at Cana and he mourned the loss of his friend Lazarus.

CHAPTER 16

THE LION AND THE LAMB

We carry within us the lion but more often than not we are called to be the lamb. The lion is majestic, fierce and powerful while the lamb is meek, mild and innocent. Jesus imitated the lamb for us all, and yet we resist it so fiercely. Though he was harshly treated, he submitted and opened not his mouth; like a lamb led to the shearers, he was silent and opened not his mouth. Isaiah 53:7.

In the Catholic Church the Good Friday service always deeply touches my soul. Nearly every year it always strikes me that as a human being I can endure hardship to a point, but there is always a breaking point: that point where I need to vent, to rant, to be heard, and to speak my piece. Perhaps after that point I can resume enduring, but inevitably for me there is a breaking point. I meditate on Good Friday, most especially on Jesus' immense suffering on the cross. He suffered on the cross after he first endured all the testing of the Pharisees, ridiculous questioning and entrapments, then false arrest. He endured a judicial system that was corrupt and had those who were not wise in power, then physical beating, humiliating disrobing and emotional jeering. He experienced such a complete lack of respect by being spit upon in the face, deprivation of sleep and food. Next, there was the physical torture of carrying the cross, the piercing throbbing pain of the crown of thorns and the crucifixion nails. His friends had abandoned him, the crowd laughed at him. He was the creator of the universe, the one who holds us in the palm of his hands, the hands we pierced. What always strikes me is that he has no breaking point. He has lost all visible power, the very people he breathes life into had deemed him worthless and insignificant. It is at this point in the meditation that I realize, EVEN IF I could make it this far without breaking, this would be the breaking point for me. This is the point where I would pop the nails out, instantly heal the wounds, clothe myself in glory and then look to THOSE PEOPLE and begin the rant. Instead, however, our God continues to endure. He endures and then in a twist none of us would have expected, he begs God the Father for forgiveness on our behalf.

We carry within us the lion but more often than not we are called to be the lamb.

Aaron desperately wanted to be the lion, as most children do, but God called him to be the lamb. When Aaron speaks of his former life, he speaks of a life that is fast and flashy, a life living on the edge, a life of fast money, cars and women, a life of "having it all." "Having it all" is the definition of the American dream. The American dream is what the goal has been for generation after generation. The media has bombarded our youth and old alike with a need for "it all." "It all" will make all your problems go away is the message we are fed, and unfortunately most of us believe it. Some may say the American dream is to be earned by hard work, blood, sweat and tears. The cynical mind sneers that being a drug dealer is not how one "earns" the American dream. Since there is no twelve-step method to the American dream, one "earns" the dream through the blood, sweat and tears which are most familiar. A child looks around, observes the method and emulates it, which is exactly what Aaron did. His method to reach the American dream did not look the same as mine because he had not shared my experience. Gratefully, my method to "having it all" was vastly different from Aaron's method, also because I had not shared his experience. Of course, modeling a life after something different than one's experience is possible and we can look back to history and name names, yet so often it does not happen that way.

"Having it all" as most of us learn the hard way, isn't really "it all." The "it all" isn't "it all" without God at the center of our lives. The blood, sweat and tears it takes to "have it all" was modeled on Calvary, which is not flashy, fast and definitely is not appealing. It is not until Easter Sunday that the reward of the blood, sweat and tears was visible. And yet, we as Christians recognize that our elementary understanding of Easter will not move to the highest level until we ourselves experience the glorious sight of heaven.

So many of us seek a life living on, or close to, the edge. We jump from planes, dive to the depths of the ocean, travel to distant lands. We are so fascinated with thrill seeking that we have become addicted to over the top reality TV. For some, living on the edge is sought through a more damaging source of drug addition, porn addiction or a life of crime. Each adrenaline high we seek next is an attempt to trump the previous thrill, all the while we are distracted from the ultimate adventure: a life lived in Christ. What could place us on the edge of our seats more than throwing all caution to the wind and saying, "God, you can have it all, you're in charge, I am following your lead?" When I think about the times I have said that prayer, I know it was the Holy Spirit leading my prayer, because even on my most courageous feeling days, I don't have that much gumption!

When we allow God to have all of us, of course without strings attached, then we are in for a real thrill. Remember Daniel in the Lion's Den? How about Daniel's three friends who survived the fiery furnace? Go to the New Testament and witness a man who turns it all over to God and suddenly a man born blind sees! The thief on the cross who finally turns it all over to God is ambushed by the love of God in the last moments of his life. Over and over again, God takes his faithful servants on adventures no writer, other than the Creator of the Universe, could compose. For those who are thrill seekers, those desiring to live life on the front lines, Jesus is the answer, every time.

Aaron frequently teaches me about true freedom. This is yet further evidence for God's ever-present force behind the prison wall and barbed wire. He quotes a song from Big Daddy Weave:

"Redeemed"

Seems like all I could see was the struggle
Haunted by ghosts that lived in my past
Bound up in shackles of all of my failures
Wondering how long is this gonna last
Then You look at this prisoner and say to me "son
Stop fighting a fight it's already been won"

I am redeemed, You set me free
So I'll shake off these heavy chains
Wipe away every stain, now I'm not who I used to be
I am redeemed
I'm redeemed

All my life I have been called unworthy
Named by the voice of my shame and regret
But when I hear you whisper, "Child lift up your head"
I remember, oh God, You're not done with me yet
I am redeemed, You set me free
So I'll shake off these heavy chains

Wipe away every stain, now I'm not who I used to be
Because I don't have to be the old man inside of me
'Cause his day is long dead and gone
Because I've got a new name, a new life I'm not the same
And a hope that will carry me home
I am redeemed, you set me free
So I'll shake off these heavy chains
Wipe away every stain, 'cause I'm not who I used to be

I am redeemed, You set me free
So I'll shake off these heavy chains
Wipe away every stain, yeah, I'm not who I used to be

Oh, God, I'm not who I used to be
Jesus, I'm not who I used to be
'Cause I am redeemed
Thank God, redeemed.

It is always hard for me to imagine Aaron in his former life, his life before he was redeemed. Even the first day I met him he described himself during his pre-incarceration years as "the worst of the worst." His turbulent childhood led to acting out in school, escalating to the point of being placed in a special classroom for children who were Behavior Disturbed. Knowing Aaron today, I can only imagine that he was a bright and energetic kid who caught on quickly. How could he have not felt anger and resentment for the childhood he was navigating alone? Aaron also is quick to describe himself as competitive. He was the star athlete when he played sports such as basketball, football and track. These are all great qualities, but without the consistent direction of an adult, it is ever so easy for the youthful mind to seek immediate gratification.

Children who experience neglect as Aaron did learn to rely on themselves. They seek quick solutions to complex problems because that is what the juvenile brain is able to compute. We refer to this as impulsive. Couldn't we all tell our own impulsive story that happened in our childhood? For most of us, we were rescued by a loving parent or teacher when our body or mouth reacted too quickly. Aaron tells the story of a day during elementary school when he brought a large sum of cash to school to impress the girls. He threw the loose bills into the air as the girls jumped double Dutch jump rope. Imagine the scene! I can almost feel the eyes of school officials pressed against office windows, parents at drop off quickly questioning their child as to who is that boy, and girls with perfect braids staring wide-eyed. When Aaron told me this story, he easily explained that at times his mother would wake his siblings and him up in the middle of the night when she returned home and give them large sums of money. Surely this felt like living, having the American dream, to the child who longed to have milk with a meal.

Fast forward to Aaron when I met him in 2016. It was easy to observe that he was wise beyond his thirty-two years; he was calm and soft spoken and undeniably full of peace and joy. Aaron had learned to take the high road of being the lamb.

CHAPTER 17

BLOOMING OUT OF SEASON

Watching a plant bloom out of season is remarkable and exciting. We take notice because it is not what we expect. Perhaps my favorite plant is the Christmas cactus. While this plant typically blooms in December, it can bloom other times of the year. Some individuals with a green thumb can even get the cactus to bloom year-round. There is a sense of pride and awe in the gardener who gets the cactus to bloom outside of December. The image of the blooming Christmas cactus comes to mind when I think of Aaron. Here is a man, accused and found guilty of a crime he professes his innocence to, in which there is a complete lack of physical evidence, then handed a devastating sentence and he in turn radiates joy?!! Aaron exemplifies blooming out of season. He radiates joy despite his struggle and challenge. If Aaron can find joy under a harsh label, an unfair judgement and an isolation from the basic comforts that most of us take for granted, then surely we too can find joy. God's mercy is endless. His love NEVER fails us. God has promised he will always be with us. More than anything, God wants our love. What is there not to be joyful about? And the best news yet, redemption is available to us all.

Aaron writes, "I bloom in this prison because I seek His face, trust Him, worship and praise, faith with actions" and later "You can tell a tree by its fruit. It bears, so I ask with a sincere heart, Father use me and keep me." Later Aaron writes, "This is where I've found peace in it all because people want to judge and compare to make themselves feel good, but you can't beat the Holy Spirit, He knows all so remain in Him." Being led by the Spirit is scary and comforting all at the same time. Speaking of his time in prison Aaron says, "There is no need to be depressed, stressed or worried none of these emotions can change the circumstance. Praying, praising and worshipping our Father in the storm is what changes and gives us faith and hope to persevere."

Praising in the storm…initially that was so difficult for me. Honestly it felt like I was pump fakin' with God; I was trembling on the inside or felt so low but I was speaking praise. I continually heard this same message: it seemed everywhere I turned I was hearing about praising God in the storm; whether it was Christian radio or my devotional or a Facebook post. I realized it was the Holy Spirit leading me. Although I didn't feel the praise in my soul at that time, the Holy Spirit was there, leading me. For me it was important to realize that even though at the time I didn't have the emotion to attach to the praise, praise in the storm was an act of trust and faith in God. As I pressed on in faith, I found over time that when I felt down, overwhelmed or anxious and I began praising God it would lift my mood and in time it began to bring a smile to my face just looking to the glory of God.

"You will know the truth and the truth will set you free!" (John 8:32). Redemption is freedom, freedom from the limitations of our human world and our human mind. Redemption is trusting and obeying the word of God even when there isn't physical evidence to back it up. Sometimes I needed to remind Aaron to "wait up for me" or "tell me that one more time" when it came to understanding God and His ways. I would joke with Aaron and yet was completely serious that he needed to remember that he had been having a 1:1 tutorial with God for the past thirteen years. He would smile, maybe even roll his eyes but he wouldn't argue with me on that. We have the invitation to get to know God on a very personal basis, but just as our God is all powerful, He is also ever gentle. God will knock at our door, but He won't beat it down. When we struggle to understand God and we want to know more, we are blessed to have the Holy

Bible to come to know him on a very intimate and personal level. I'll be the first person to say the Bible can be intimidating and confusing. Yet we are reminded to live in community and to care for one another; sharing scripture with one another is just that.

Living in community can be a blessing and a challenge all at the same time. I know I'm getting a lot of Amens on that, especially if you have ever served on a church committee, you know exactly what I am talking about. As citizens of the community, the body of Christ, we must stay attached to the vine. At times the voices of the world, those around us, and even our own church traditions are so loud and confusing it is hard to discern the voice of God. What are we to do? First we pray. That, after all, is our lifeline to God. We surround ourselves with people who first and foremost have a personal relationship with God. You will know someone has a personal relationship with Jesus when you see their words and actions lining up. Some of the people I know who have a personal relationship with God have never used that verbiage; they didn't have to; their actions and the peace and joy on their faces told me. Sadly, the opposite is also true. Remember the Pharisees; we still experience Pharisees today. Don't we all know the person who is so good at following all the rules and yet, they just don't get it? Yes, these people can be found in the church, too. A few years back I was teaching religious education and on this particular night another teacher who was very active and very much in a leadership role within the church pointed to the cross and preached to the children that Jesus died because of THEIR sins. So much of what she was saying was right, yet she missed the premise Jesus died for OUR sins, and most relevant to my relationship with God, he died for ME! When we begin to comprehend that Jesus stretched out his arms, suffered excruciating pain and immense humiliation for ME, that is a game changer. We begin to understand that we have been bought at a price we cannot repay. We don't deserve it. We can't earn it. We can accept it and live our lives humbly in service and love for the one who gave all for ME.

Jesus calls us to walk that same road he walked: a road of humility and a road of service. It is not an easy road, certainly not a paved road. Sometimes our car breaks down on the road and at times visibility is so low as we forge ahead in the worst of storms. However, just as a winding country road can be dicey in the winter, it can be peaceful in the summer. One never knows what you will find around the next curve in the road. Sometimes we approach the curve too fast and, as I remember from learning to drive on gravel country roads, taking the curve too fast will spin you out of control and possibly land you in the cornfield. So the road is traveled at a steady pace, trusting that we will reach our destination even when the corn of late summer is too high to see the end of the road. At times the road seems lonely and then out of nowhere another traveler will pass with a wave of encouragement. It is not a fast freeway, but rather a trip worthy of our attention and diligence.

On August 12, 2017, Heather Heyer, a thirty-two-year-old woman from Virginia, decided to take the road less traveled on that Saturday morning. Instead of sleeping in or enjoying a lazy summer morning at home, she chose the road of humility. She stood in attendance opposing a White Nationalist Rally in Charlottesville, Virginia. She would stand on the side of love and she would take her Saturday morning to give to those who did not have the luxury of privilege that surrounded her. What Heyer did not know on that morning as she left her home was that at the end of her day her life on this earth would be over and she would be referred to as a martyr. In her humble giving she would open so many closed eyes to see that racism was not just ugly and offensive to the victims but also to those who witnessed it. Heyer never sought to be famous or known and yet her last decision to attend a rally would become her defining moment. Her simple choice to stand on the side of love and stare into the face of hate would be her most lasting memory.

Heather Heyer would not be the first of the martyrs for the cause of racism. There had been so many in the recent past. Maybe it was the thought of Sandra Bland, or Philandro Castile that gave a sense of urgency to her decision to attend the rally. Maybe it was the ache of Tamir Rice. Maybe it was simply her tie to humanity, the innate knowledge that we are all interconnected, that we are our brother's keeper. Maybe she was motivated to stand with love because she could sense the death grip that hate had on us. Heather Heyer did not attend the rally for herself; she stepped out of her comfort zone and used her position of white privilege to show whoever happened to notice that there was more to her life than her own comfort. As it would turnout on this particular day, the whole country would notice. Sadly, it would take the shedding of white blood to wake up America and sustain attention in the headlines.

CHAPTER 18

WHAT JESUS TOLD US ABOUT THE POOR BUT WE DIDN'T GET

Boldly and truthfully Pope Francis stated during a weekly homily to a general audience, "To ignore the poor is to despise God." Whoa! There certainly is no misinterpreting that statement, and certainly for most of us, it abruptly calls us to examine our conscience, likely showing us something ugly. Pew Research Center found in 2011 that 56 percent of Americans were living in the high-income category, which accounted for only 7 percent globally. Those in this elite high-income group were defined as those living on more than $50 a day in 2011.

When you know you are living in the top 7 percent globally and yet you continue to live like you are doing all you can to help the poor, Pope Francis statement calls you out. We find that there are so many poor around us and yet often we ignore them and rationalize that they want to be that way or that they are not helping themselves. It is very hard to help yourself when you are a child in poverty. Wasn't this the case for Aaron and his siblings? Wasn't it ultimately hunger that contributed to their need to earn money at an age as young as fifth grade? It is so easy to condemn being a drug dealer as a filthy despicable way to earn a living and yet don't we smugly ask, "Why don't they help themselves?" It seems to me, if you are a hungry eleven-year-old, you look to the people around you and see how they are earning money. If drug dealing has been modeled for you, that is what you know and that is what you do.

Repeatedly, we hear Jesus reach out to the poor, call them blessed and take time for them. He demonstrates over and over that the poor are precious in the eyes of God. Not only did Jesus call us to the poor, he came as a poor homeless man born to a young unwed mother. Did we forget that?

Why then are the poor not only not precious in our eyes but shunned and despised? We can say, "Ah, we are human, it is the way of the world." Both of which are true statements, and yet as Christians we are called to live not by the rules of this world but by the law of God. How often we cringe in our pews when the reading at church is of the rich young man who is called to sell everything and give it to the poor? Why? Because deep down we know that is a reading we need to hear and should live, but to do so would look so drastic and weird. Drastic and weird, hmmm. That sounds so very familiar. I must admit when I hear about John the Baptist eating locusts and honey wandering around in the desert wearing burlap, the thought of drastic and weird are not far behind. Drastic and weird. Drastic and weird according to whose standards and doesn't it take drastic and weird to get our fleeting attention? Don't actions speak louder than words?

Our faith must be put into action. We must move beyond the profession of our faith and actually live it. Never once did Jesus tell us it would be easy, and certainly his life was not easy. Yet we continue to look for what is comfortable and easy.

Hearing Aaron's story and then coming to know him as a person was not easy. It called me to examine how we function as a society. More personally, it called me to look at my own judgements and convictions that I falsely placed on others, turning my back to those in need. I had seen the face of injustice and, more than a face, a friend. It's easy to walk away from an overwhelming complex social issue, but abandoning a friend tears at your heart. When we keep the poor, the underprivileged, the outcasts of our society on the fringes it is very easy to walk away. God calls us to action! If we truly believe in the living body of Christ on this earth then we need to act like it.

Our obsession with worldly success and our fleeting attention will always try to distract us and talk us out of engaging with the poor and underprivileged. To truly live as the body of Christ we must purposefully place ourselves in the midst of the poor and underprivileged. We must take the time to get to know not just the people who are easy to love and get to know. Christian love is a greater calling. Christian love calls us to uncomfortable situations, but we serve a God who is a great gift giver; He will not be outdone. When we give to God, he returns with gifts a hundred-fold. When I am having a bad day and I am feeling down, the best way to ease those feelings is to give to another. It works every time! God calls us to reach outside of our own feelings and circumstances and enter into the struggles of another, not to complete our Christian duty, but to transform our lives.

"Love is the only force capable of transforming an enemy into a friend," Martin Luther King, Jr. As Christians we have heard thousands of times that God is love. Have you ever wondered what that really meant? Have you ever wondered what that would ultimately look like? Perhaps it would look like the forgiveness from the heart of Immaculee Ilibagiza, a Rwandan genocide survivor. Immaculee survived the genocide by hiding in a bathroom for three months, crammed into the three-by-four-foot space with seven other women; while hearing the bloodcurdling screams of her family and neighbors as they were hunted down and killed. Today the peaceful soul of Immaculee speaks globally, sharing her message of forgiveness. Immaculee understands that love is the only force capable of transforming former enemies into friends, as she embraces and forgives her fellow countrymen.

Scientists recently stated that any two humans on this earth share 99.9 percent of the same genetic makeup. If we are 99.9 percent alike, why are we concentrating so heavily on our differences? As Christians we believe that our best life is a life in Christ. A life in the body of Christ includes each and every soul on this planet. Until our hearts break with empathy and love for our neighbor, we will not have peace within regions, countries or our own hearts. Listen to how Aaron describes his current situation of false imprisonment, "Yes I've been falsely accused and I truly thank God for it, because I was literally saved from condemnation and hell eternally. I am remorseful at the thought of this person (his accuser) being used to do this, so I pray for her salvation, but no one needs to feel sorry for me. I am at peace, I see and hear clearly."

We all have something to give the world, no matter what our financial situation is: wealthy, financially stable, living pay check to pay check or impoverished. Kindness costs nothing other than time, and as my mom likes to say, "We all have twenty-four hours in a day." I want to share with you now one of my most treasured memories.

What makes a meal amazing? I'm talking about the kind of amazing that is so memorable your taste buds water at the thought of it. For most of us we can remember a meal like this. Sometimes I wonder if it is the food or the company that makes it so amazing; undoubtedly it's both. Have you heard it said that food made with love tastes better? Maybe that question brought to mind Grandma's pie, or Mom's tamales, or Dad's barbecue.

My family and I experienced one of these amazing meals while we were on vacation in Guatemala in the summer of 2015. We had decided to take a tour which included climbing a volcano for the day. The tour included lunch at the top of the volcano which sounded absolutely amazing and memorable. It turned out the marketing description in the excursion brochure couldn't even come close to explaining how wonderful the experience would be. Excitedly, we loaded buses in the morning that drove us for about one hour into a more rural part of Guatemala to a community living at the base of a volcano. The volcano had erupted five years earlier and destroyed all the homes at the base. The families that resided there had tried over the past five years to piece their lives back together. Due to the fact that they were living in a rural area, access to materials to reconstruct their homes was limited and the materials were even more expensive than they would've been if they lived in the city. Even if these families would have had the materials closer, they lacked the financial resources to purchase materials to fully reconstruct their homes.

Homes in this area consisted of structures which had perhaps two cement block walls with a piece of tin as a roof. Some families were less fortunate and had the side of the mountain as a wall and pieces of tarp and sticks to serve as shelter. Earning a living in these rural areas was very limited as well, due to lack of transportation to the city, poor farming ground on the side of the mountain, and lack of financial resources to start businesses. Families that lived at the base of the volcano worked as porters to assist tourists up the volcano. They rented their horses daily to tourists to have the opportunity to ride a horse up the volcano. The horse was the livelihood of the family; therefore, a man or a young boy from the household would serve as a guide walking alongside the horse.

The fact that we wimpy Americans actually contemplated hiking instead of riding the horse is very comical in hindsight. The volcano was extremely steep and had very rugged terrain. Once we had mounted our horses and begun to ascend the volcano, we were very grateful we had made the decision to ride horses. However, it did not take long and the reality of the situation began to settle in my soul. Here I was, this privileged American, riding, while this man dressed in tattered clothes and shoes that were falling apart completed the four-hour hike on foot to the summit. As our altitude increased, the air was thinner and dryer, making all of us very thirsty. Along the way were stations to purchase beverages. These were eagerly purchased and we quickly…greedily…drank the water we had purchased from the previous station. After finishing my water and wiping my brow atop my horse, my eyes drifted down to Pedro who was walking along not complaining of his worn shoes, still wearing a smile on his face, concerned about my comfort. The leader of the guides carried a backpack on his back which carried our lunch for the picnic at the top of the volcano. He was happy and expressed pride at the fact that he had managed to pack a gluten-free lunch which my daughter and I required. In order to accomplish this, he had to stray from the usual sandwiches for lunch. He explained that his wife had gotten up early that morning and made tortillas, which were still warm in his backpack. As the terrain got steeper, the guides shared the responsibility of carrying the backpack. With much prompting I was able to finally convince them to let me hold the backpack atop my horse.

As we continued up the volcano it came to my awareness that there was no way there was enough food in the backpack for my family and all the guides to eat lunch. They did not have money to buy drinks along the way either, so the reality began to set into my brain that we would reach our destination and our guides would not have anything to eat or drink. This awareness within me turned from sadness, to guilt, to panic. How could I eat this lunch in front of them and know that they were hungry? And yet, the other question in my brain was, how could I not? They had anticipated our day and were eager to share this meal with us. However, they would not be sharing, but just providing. I realized it would be rude not to eat the lunch. The language barrier was too great for me to be able to explain my concerns, and then there was the case of their pride.

As it turns out, once the meal was laid out and we guest tourists had a chance to eat, then the guides ate, too. While it still did not feel fair or right, I knew that was what they desired so that we could have an enjoyable day. They desired for us to experience their country and culture authentically. I can say without a doubt that it was the best meal I have ever had. Now, of course the beautiful view my family enjoyed atop the volcano contributed to this. However, the one fact that made this meal absolutely terrific and memorable was the sacrifice that was put into making the meal. It was a sacrifice that showed the love that they had for us as visitors to their country. It was the sacrifice of the mother who got up early at 4:00 a.m. to make tortillas for us. It was the sacrifice of the men who walked the horses to ensure our comfort. It was the sacrifice of the extra weight on their backs as they carried food and drink up the rugged terrain. I thank God that I had the opportunity to experience this meal. I was grateful to have the opportunity to see the sacrifice and understand the sacrifice that was put into providing this meal for me and my family.

Each Sunday, my family and I are invited to an amazing meal, the Eucharist. How many times had I failed to see the sacrifice? How many times had I failed to realize who I was really sharing the meal with? Did I even consider all the preparation and sacrifice that was put into this meal for me?

When I sat upon the horse, I was concerned that I did not want to appear to be the ugly American. I did not want to be the ungrateful tourist. I was concerned about the comfort of my guide and his hunger was foremost in my mind. However, when I came to the Eucharist each Sunday, I think when I reflect back, that I was the ugly Christian. I was callous; I was rushed; I was late; I was inattentive; I was preoccupied with the events of the day to come.

CHAPTER 19

OBEDIENCE AND MERCY

I desire mercy not sacrifice.
—Matthew 12:7

Mercy is a word that requires definition. Mercy is giving a pass when it isn't deserved or warranted. Mercy is the free gift of compassion from someone in a position of power to the one who has no power. We all desire that God be merciful to us. When we are truly honest, the mercy of God is our lifeline; it's all we have to stand on. Of course, we must have faith, but even with the best of faith, without the mercy of God we are hopeless. Then comes that line, you know the one, likely it makes you cringe as much as it does me, "Forgive us our trespasses as we forgive those who trespass against us." So the very mercy we seek is the mercy we are called to give; the mercy we receive is the mercy we give? As stated in an earlier chapter, Anthony Esolen teaches us, mercy costs us in sweat and time.

Reverend Mike Schmitz describes that kind of mercy as the understanding that "you only really love Jesus as much as the person you can't stand the most." I don't know about you but that statement is like a sucker punch to the gut. That makes me bow any arrogant hairs that stand defiant on my head; I have work to do! Is that the level of humility that is needed to end racism and white privilege? Certainly that is a starting point to finding a solution. I can never end racism and remove the power of white privilege by shaking my finger in blame. I can impact racism by teaching with words and actions, but those words and actions must be done in love.

We must look again at Martin Luther King, Jr.'s quote, "Love is the only force capable of transforming an enemy into a friend." How often do we feel most insulted and persecuted when our friends or family are spoken of in a negative manner? Is it not innate to want to stand up and defend them? What would our world look like if we believed what Jesus told us, that we are the body of Christ and we are our brother's keeper? How quickly could we resolve our racial and cultural differences if we armed ourselves with the true love, which only comes from God and multiplies with prayer and fasting?

When we take a chance to get to know people then there is no room for assumptions. The perfect example of this was my friendship with my next-door neighbor, who lived across the hall from my apartment. She was a Libyan immigrant who was Muslim. She and her family had fled their war-torn country after having experienced the war firsthand. The experience of war had traumatized her four-year-old son and he was experiencing PTSD. Unfortunately, we lived very close to the airport, so when the airplanes would fly overhead the young boy would scream in terror, anticipating bombs. Had I not known why he was screaming, it would have been easy for me to jump to the conclusion that "those Muslim people were being abusive to their poor innocent child." I could have easily confirmed the media's proclamation of the Muslim that is violent, the Muslim that is angry, and the Muslim that is not like me. Instead my heart ached and I offered a prayer for my friend and her son. It also called me to a higher level of patience with my own children, as I never heard her raise her voice, no matter how high pitched and how frequent the screams were.

Animals in nature can teach us great lessons: remember the lessons of the buffalo herd who stood with its weakest and most vulnerable member. Silence condones wrongdoings; we must stand with the most vulnerable.

CHAPTER 20

WALKING ON WATER

We will know we are living in the kingdom when our prayers, become more about Him and less about us. Our prayers will then transcend to our lives and instead of our lives being about us, as we submit to the will of God, we want what He wants more and more; our lives become about Him. As we let go of us, we gain Him. It sounds simple, and yet it is a great and constant challenge for us, because we are surrounded by loud flashy distractions. The world around us constantly sends us the message to watch out for ourselves, then protect our family, and stand for our country. This message just doesn't come from the obvious media outlets but perhaps the strongest most convincing voice is the voice of our trusted friends and family. We hear things like: "If you don't look out for you who will?" "Take care of yourself first or you can't help anyone else," "If anyone deserves it, it's you." If I apply these statements to my relationship with God, then they are true, but more often I have found myself using them as an excuse. The truth is, I am just as guilty of making statements like these to my friends and family.

Meeting Aaron changed me in so many ways. Mostly I just wanted to know more about this source of peace and joy that he found in an overcrowded prison, placed there by a horrific mistake or a very devious setup. Oddly, the how or what that put Aaron in prison wasn't his greatest life story to tell. It was God, all God. God had redeemed Aaron. God had picked him up from the lowest of low places and showed him the power of His Spirit placed within Aaron's humble self. Not only did God reveal himself to Aaron, but God empowered Aaron with the authority that only God can give, to preach His holy word. Only God could allow Aaron to be completely free even if he was limited in this world by a physical prison. God wants that for all of us. He desires us to ascend to live in his presence even as we walk this earth.

Inner peace and joy not dependent on what the world can provide is so alluring. As young girls, my mother taught my sisters and me the value of an education. "Get a good education; that can never be taken away from you." I love this and it still resonates with me today. It is something that I pass on to my own girls. Yet working as an Occupational Therapist, I know all too well that your education can be taken away. Trauma or disease can attack our complex yet delicate brains, interrupting the basic neuro-connections and disabling all we hold as constant and certain. So while I teach my girls to value education and expect them to put forth full effort, I tell them, "Get to know God on a personal level, because no matter where you are or what happens to you in life, God will be with you." Even if the brain cannot send neurological connections to speak prayers, sing praise or raise your arms in Halleluiah, the heart can speak love and seek the source of love, that which is God Almighty.

I venture to say that all of us will reach a point in our life where we will have only God to lean on. For Aaron it was a prison cell, for me a hospital bed, and still others will reach that point surrounded by people and yet completely alone. Who will be there with you when you hit rock bottom? God will be there. God who created you, who knows all your history: the good, the bad and the ugly. He is the same God who will be there to carry you to the top of the mountain and celebrate the victory with you. True peace is more than just coexisting; it is living in God's love every moment.

Taking the risk and trusting in God, going into territory that is not the safe and known path, is only possible with faith. Aaron refers to this action as stepping out of the boat. Once we are out of the boat we need to keep our eyes on Jesus or we start to sink, just as Peter started to sink when he was called to walk on the water with Jesus.

Imagine how completely thrilling it must have been to be Peter, walking on water!! While like Peter, there are so many times that I am paralyzed with fear, when we step out of the boat we are immediately responding to the call of God. Stepping out of the boat is an immediate act of obedience. God calls us to tasks that are completely impossible if we attempt them on our own strength and understanding, but when we respond to God with immediate obedience we are acting in pure faith. If Peter, who had direct conversations with Jesus, heard his teachings and saw his miracles day after day for three years, had moments of doubt and denial, we can expect the same challenges. However, just as we can expect the same challenges, we also have the gift of continual invitation to walk on the water with Jesus. The vastness of the availability of Jesus to us is forever awe-inspiring. His love for us stands firm despite our wavering faith.

God was with Aaron the day he was arrested and God will be with him the day he walks out of prison. It is the constant love of God that has not only sustained Aaron's sanity and spirit for the past thirteen years, but that is the source of his transformation. If we understand that God is humble, peaceful, patient and loving, we will understand that those qualities are characteristics that lead to a fuller deeper relationship with Him.

CHAPTER 21

PRAYER LEADS US TO OUR HEART'S GREATEST DESIRES

Our heart's greatest desire is God. Prayer is where it all begins: that is how we begin to have a relationship with God. Yet for many, the thought of prayer can be overwhelming and intimidating. I have had many people comment that they do not know how to pray. This is paralyzing, because prayer is the key to a personal relationship with God. Prayer is how we come to know God. The myths and truths of prayer are vast, as is the literature to guide us and lead us. For many, early on we were taught that prayer was reciting certain words in a certain order. Perhaps you have heard that if you sing, you are praying twice. Of course, then there is the advice to just talk to God, which undoubtedly leads to the question of what does God want me to talk to Him about?

I think for many people a prayer life begins in a desperate hour. At a loved one's bedside, when our own lives are at risk, or when we find ourselves in situations that we have no idea how to get out of. Equally, many of us are guilty of wiping the sweat from our brow and skipping along when the urgent need is gone. A quality prayer life is one in which we invest time and give God our best on a consistent basis. Yes, prayers can be elaborate and eloquent, but they can also be simple. No matter how we participate in prayer, what matters initially is that we participate. Prayer is the door through which we pass to know God. Knowing God leads to loving God, and from there out of love we serve Him, because He becomes what our hearts desire the most.

I believe that there are a multitude of ways in which we can pray and have personal communication with God. We start where we are able, where we are comfortable, always remembering that God already knows our hearts. I like to remember to thank God, praise God, ask forgiveness from God, and lastly, petition God.

Thanking God: I like to start easy. There is always an abundance to be thankful for, oftentimes as we list one thing, ten more come to mind. Thanksgiving quickly becomes praise. Praising God comes from a joyful, grateful heart that is steered by the grace of the Holy Spirit within us. The breath of God that runs through our body will teach us how to come into relationship with Him, if only we take the time to be with God in prayer.

Asking forgiveness requires us to have a spark of humility. That spark will ignite and grow as our relationship with God grows. God already knows the worst parts of us, wouldn't we feel better if we cleared the air and laid all our sin on the table? He already knows it anyway!

Sometimes my daughters struggle with asking forgiveness when they have done wrong. The philosophy being that I, being their mother, know what has been done wrong and being their mother, I understand that they didn't intend the offense. Many times my daughters require prompting in asking forgiveness. What my daughters do not fully comprehend is that until they seek reconciliation, they have not taken responsibility for their actions. The same is true of our relationship with God. If we excuse our behavior away with the circumstances of our life and presume that God knows our struggles and our hearts, there is an awkwardness, an obstacle to full communion with God. In the case of my daughters, they avoid me when they have done wrong. They keep their distance, hoping that I will forget their errors. I must admit that like my daughters, I have been guilty of avoiding God, hoping that enough time will pass and my offense will be forgotten. Perhaps you have played the game like this: I will try to make up for my wrongdoing, smooth everything over and get a pass on the admitting I was wrong and asking forgiveness part. This doesn't work either, because just as when we try to smooth things over without discussing the issue with a friend or family member, it continues to resurface until we address it. Have you ever had the experience of having multiple opportunities to learn the same life lesson? I like to joke that some of us, primarily me, are slower learners than others. Some of us need lessons repeated and repeated. Could that repetition be due to the fact that we refused to take responsibility and address the problem head on?

Once we have given thanks and praise and have asked for forgiveness, then we are in a place to petition. We can petition with sincerity and humility. We find ourselves in a place where our petitions are less important because we feel the love of our Creator and we trust that He knows our needs and has our best interest in mind. As our prayer lives evolve, we will come to the realization that our prayers are more about what God desires than what we desire, because His gifts, His plans are always better than ours.

I close this chapter with a prayer Aaron wrote to me: "Father, Abba, your presence is evident, we thank you with a sincere heart, knowing your will and word will be established. You are all powerful, you're the greatest King, you are miracle, you are love, you are joy, you are peace, and you are in us, through our only comforter the Holy Spirit. Holy Spirit you are free to dwell in us, speak through us, heal through us, we are humbled by your willingness to be one with us, You Father YAHWEH Reign forever, I trust you today, I have faith, unmovable faith in you today. In Yeshua Jesus the Messiah's name, Amen."

CHAPTER 22

FORGIVENESS

"As I walked out the door toward my freedom, I
knew that if I did not leave all the anger, hatred
and bitterness behind, I would still be in prison"
~Nelson Mandela

One of the many things that is shocking and amazing about
Aaron is that he is not bitter or full of hatred. This is so shocking not
only because of the huge voids from his childhood, but also the fact
that he is incarcerated for rape, such an ugly and despicable crime, of
which he professes his innocence, as he has for thirteen years. Maybe
it was the peace within him and the joy that he radiates that made me
want to know him more. In order to come to peace and joy, forgiveness had to come first. Among all the people who had hurt Aaron and
the system that had failed him, perhaps the one who Aaron needed to
forgive most was himself.

Aaron's incredible peace and joy led me to ask him about forgiveness. When I was all fired up with the shooting of Black man
after Black man by police, Aaron was at peace. When I loathed all
the ignorant people who tried to say that somehow each man was at
fault, Aaron nodded in agreement that they were wrong, but he still
had joy in his heart which radiated out of him peacefully. So what
was that, I kept asking myself? How could he patiently wait in prison
without anger and resentment? How did he get to that place? I knew

the answer was in his relationship with God, but in all my prayers and all my study of seeking God, I had not found how to resolve my contempt for injustice.

I asked Aaron to write to me about forgiveness and here is what he sent me:

> "In all honesty, the word forgiveness sounds like something you don't want to do. It's equivalent to hearing jump off a bridge or out of a plane without a parachute. A little dramatic, but so true. Which in turn reminds your soul that this commandment comes from a higher existence, which is our Creator, Yahweh. Your flesh automatically was with that word; however, we must comply because it is beneficial or even life-saving. More importantly, Jesus directly speaks to forgiveness in Matthew 6:14: "For if you forgive others their transgressions (sins), your heavenly Father will also forgive you." One of the greatest stories in the Bible of forgiveness is Joseph forgiving his brothers for what they did by selling him for twenty pieces of silver to the Ishmaelites:
>
> Genesis 37:23–28
>
> So when Joseph came up to his brothers, they stripped him of his tunic, the long, ornamented tunic he had on; then they took him and threw him into the cistern. The cistern was empty; there was no water in it. Then they sat down to eat. Looking up, they saw a caravan of Ishmaelites coming from Gilead, their camels laden with gum, balm and resin to be taken down into Egypt. Judah said to his brothers: "What is to be gained by killing our brother and concealing his blood? Come let us sell him to these

Ishmaelites, instead of doing away with him ourselves. After all, he is our brother, our own flesh." His brothers agreed. Midianite traders passed by, and they pulled Joseph out of the cistern. They sold Joseph for twenty pieces of silver to the Ishmaelites, who took him to Egypt.

Time passes and Joseph meets his brothers in Egypt when they are desperate and in need. From Joseph's position of power he addresses his brothers who sold him:

Genesis 45:4–5

"Come closer to me," Joseph told his brothers. When they had done so, he said: "I am your brother Joseph whom you sold into Egypt. But now do not be distressed, and do not be angry with yourselves for having sold me here. It was really for the sake of saving lives that God sent me here ahead of you."

As startling as this is, clearly this is a message that God wants us to grasp. Again we see in the New Testament this same level of forgiveness, but this time from our God. First in the Parable of the Prodigal Son:

Luke 15:11–32

A man had two sons and the younger son said to the father, "Father, give me the share of your estate that should come to me." So the father divided the property between them. After a few days the younger son collected all his belongings and set off to a distant country where he squandered his inheritance on a life of dissipation. When he had freely spent everything, a severe famine struck the country, and he found himself in dire need. So he hired himself out to one of the local citizens who sent him to his farm to tend the swine. And he longed to eat his fill of the pods on which the swine fed, but nobody gave him any. Coming to his senses he thought, "How many of my father's hired workers have more than enough food to eat, but here I am dying of hunger. I shall get up and go to my father and I shall say to him, "Father, I have sinned against heaven and against you. I no longer deserve to be called your son; treat me as you would treat one of your hired workers. So he got up and went back to his father. While he was still a long way off, his father caught sight of him, and was filled with compassion. He ran to his son, embraced him and kissed him. His son said to him, "Father, I have sinned against heaven and against you: I no longer deserve to be called your son." But his father ordered his servants, "Quickly bring the finest robe and put it on him: put a ring on his finger and sandals on his feet. Take the fattened calf and slaughter it. Then let us celebrate with a feast, because this son of mine was dead, and has come to life again: he was lost, and has been found." Then the celebration began. Now the older son had been out in the field and, on his way back, as he neared the house, he heard the sound of music and dancing. He called one of the servants and asked what this might mean. The servant said to him, "Your brother has returned and your father has slaughtered the fattened calf because he has him back safe and sound." He became angry, and when he refused to enter the house, his father came out and pleaded with him. He said to his father in reply, "Look at all those years I served you and not once did I disobey your orders; yet you never even gave me a young goat to feast on with my friends. But when your son returns who swallowed up your property with prostitutes, for him you slaughter the fattened calf." He said to him, "My son, you are here with me always, everything I have is yours. But now we must celebrate and rejoice, because your brother was dead and has come to life again; he was lost and has been found."

In this parable, Jesus illustrates the Father's love for us shown in mercy and forgiveness when we sin. We see how generous and compassionate our Father truly is. Jesus clearly and directly speaks to us about forgiveness in Matthew 6:14–15: If you forgive others their transgressions, your heavenly Father will forgive you. But if you do not forgive others, neither will your Father forgive your transgressions.

Then as Jesus suffers on the cross, we see that love poured out yet again. Jesus hangs in humiliation and agony and powerfully steps outside of his own misery and pleads to the Father when he says, "Forgive them Father for they know not what they do." He pleads for the congregation who has desired his blood to be spilled. When Jesus states: "they know not what they do," he simply highlights that the reason he came down from his glorious throne was to lay his life down. It pleased the Father to see him suffer for the world, because of Jesus' unprecedented obedience which is our example of complete trust and love for the Father. This is the very same world that disrespects, rejects and disregards His Holiness. "Forgive them," Jesus pleads in his horrific suffering.

Aaron describes his own journey of forgiveness. While it is true that he is imprisoned for a crime he maintains his innocence of, he is able to recognize his transgressions outside of this conviction. He says, "I forgave myself first, for being a person who loved to sin at one time and for the sins I've committed." He goes on to say that forgiving yourself is everything: the first huge step to real recovery.

Aaron says the next step is to forgive those who sinned against you. He describes a process of picturing the person's face in your mind and going back to the offense and allowing yourself to acknowledge the feelings you felt when the trespassing took place. Aaron's next step is to search your heart and truly apply the blood of the Lamb to the altercation or situation.

No doubt this is not an easy or quick process. Certainly it sounds painful and effortful. Aaron advises what to do when you feel yourself struggling with forgiving others: "I've learned that the easiest way to forgive others is to remember all the things you want to be forgiven for. This helps you to not unrighteously judge others also."

Oftentimes I would find myself struggling with forgiving someone who had done something very minor to me or hurt someone that I loved. I could mull it over in my mind time and time again, nurse it year after year and hold onto it; all the while the only one it was hurting was myself. I believe many of us find ourselves in this situation. Sometimes it is family members that are most difficult to forgive after they have hurt us. In Aaron's case, the very people who were supposed to protect him the most, hurt him the most: his parents. And yet, he has found the ability to forgive them and love them in their weakness.

I could follow Aaron's process of forgiveness but I always found myself getting stuck on the act that seemed unforgivable. What about terrible atrocities like genocide? Sins in which entire groups of people demonstrated complete disregard for entire groups of people, including children? I thought to myself, "I don't know how I can forgive that." What about premeditated plans of destruction and complicated lies that are solely for a person's own benefit at the expense of another?

My eyes scrolled down the paper of Aaron's letter to me, and my eyes widened and fixed on the sentence, "I forgive the slave owners that unjustly abused people of color. I forgive those who sold my ancestors to the highest bidder, removing them from their homeland and families. I forgive those who assigned my ancestors to hard labor for little money or no money at all. I forgive everyone and everything that is considered wrong, by God Almighty's standards."

What?! Even I had not forgiven my ancestors who had been the slave owners. As a matter of fact, like most white people I knew, I wanted to distance myself as far away from them as I could. Perhaps that was the problem: when I stood vigilantly judging others, I had no time to look inward. Perhaps I felt I had no need to look inward. Here was my friend, a Black man, a victim of mass incarceration, forgiving slave owners, going back to where it all started.

Perhaps you are wondering if Aaron was able to forgive those who put him in prison. What about the woman who accused him? Her accusation had so far cost him thirteen years of his life. Was that forgivable? He explains that he does forgive his accuser; in fact, he says he prays for her. "I have truly forgiven everyone involved because we all have come short and fall short of the glory of God. I have a Jesus' point of view on life situations." He further explains, "I was a sinner on my way to eternal fire and now I'm being used to snatch others out of the fire. Only God can write that story." "When it comes to people's judgements remember no one has a Heaven or a Hell they can send you to. Jesus said I'm forgiven so I don't have to convince anyone else. This is where I have found peace through it all, because people want to judge or compare to make themselves feel good, but you can't beat the (feeling of peace from) Holy Spirit. He knows all. So remain in him and him in you! Amen!"

Which is why Aaron can say with confidence, "I sleep perfect at night, having my heart and mind set in this place. I've been released from that prison that so many people that are not locked in a cell are not free from." "I'm very aware that many people who are out roaming the world are not truly free but are imprisoned or confined, more so than a person who is physically confined in a prison cell, because they will not forgive. They wake up every morning to what they did or what someone has done to them." Aaron closes with, "We might take God at his word, when he says he forgives us and remember that Jesus laid down his life and was risen all for the purpose of forgiveness."

The depth of our relationship with God has more to do with our acceptance of mercy and our willingness to ask forgiveness than it does with how little or how much we sin. We cannot earn heaven.

That is a reality we have to accept and a gift that we have to embrace. This life is not about us, but about Him, and it is only in Him that we will find true peace and freedom. That is His gift and our choice.

Another critical part of forgiveness is repentance. Pastor Tony Nolan defines repentance as that moment when you stop arguing with God about your sin and agree with Him. Repentance is unpopular. It can be hard work and it requires dedication. We all want to be forgiven but doing our part to make amends seems like one more thing on our to-do list, or maybe it's a reminder to us of that which we don't want to be reminded of. It is easy to fool ourselves into believing that saying we are sorry is enough, that we don't really have to repent or that simply the act of saying we are sorry is repentance. Repentance is putting our words into action.

Family life always presents many lessons in asking for and accepting forgiveness. I noticed with my own girls that it was easy for them to ask forgiveness but then making amends was the hard part. We can all think of a time a child is told to tell another child they are sorry and the apology seems to be spat out of the mouth and body language and tone of voice do not relay a convicted heart. I have had discussions with my girls about their need to demonstrate the sincerity of their heart with making amends. Making amends proves to the injured party that the transgressor is truly remorseful and desires to right the relationship.

One of the best ways we can repent to God is fasting or self-denial. Fasting, which is also not such a popular concept, has deep biblical roots in both the old and new testaments. John the Baptist fasts in the desert, Jesus fasted for forty days, the disciples are seen fasting in Acts and so fasting is to be a part of who we are. Fasting strengthens us spiritually to resist the temptations all around us.

After we establish a life of prayer and fasting, we will begin to see God everywhere we look. Prayer and fasting strengthen us and God rewards our desire to know him by revealing Himself to us. The strength we get from a solid foundation in Christian practices that date back to our ancestors of the Old Testament will allow us to faithfully turn to God, obeying his commands and trusting in his providence.

CHAPTER 23

LIVING IN GOD'S WILL: OUR BEST PLAN

Aaron describes that we must realize that our steps have already been ordained by the Father; the Father knows what we will do before we make the move. If we stay in the word, following the commands our Father has clearly given us, no matter what the trial or tribulation, we are not alone. Aaron writes me, "Our Father knows the sincerity of your heart and your prayers are believable true and dear to him. More prayers should be from the mind of knowing it's done; before you pray know it is done already."

"Lord, you have probed me, you know me: you know when I sit and stand; you understand my thoughts from afar. You sift through my travels and my rest; with all my ways you are familiar. Even before a word is on my tongue, Lord, you know it all" (Psalm 139:2–4).

As humans, we often struggle to give meaning to our lives. We search and search and search. Our purpose will be found in doing the will of God. It is not only our purpose but our responsibility to give our life to the one who gave us our first breath and then died to give us eternal life. Yet our gentle loving God does not oblige us to this commitment, but seeks our earnest desire to trust Him enough to turn to our Father and cry out in need, offering our life as the only gift we can give in love. The one and only desire our Father has for us is for us to be in relationship with Him and love Him. When we love Him, we trust Him. When we trust Him, we want more of Him and when we want more we suddenly recognize that receiving comes from giving our life away to the one who gave it first to us.

The mystery of life is about embarking on the unknown, which we can only do with faith and trust. If we do not have faith and trust we are stuck in cycles of anxiety and depression. We have to let go of the control to experience the gift of life in its fullest form. Isn't it odd, though, that we often don't grasp this lesson until our back is against the wall and we have run out of other options? Imagine how great it is when we are fully functioning, living in peace, enjoying life and yet able to choose trust. That would be true freedom. We would not be choosing trust because our backs are against the wall and we had nowhere else to turn, but because we had the wisdom and insight to know that this was our best choice. Don't miss His calling; it's the only way you are truly free.

When I looked back at my struggles with Lyme disease, I realized that I was continually counting on myself to find a solution. My medical knowledge would help me to understand literature. If that wasn't enough, I had the financial resources to seek doctors who were specialists. In the end I would travel to five states seeking medical advice. Sure, I was praying along the way, but, I didn't really "need" God, at least not just yet. I would lean on my self-determination to persevere through harsh diets in attempts to cleanse my body of the bacteria. I learned that scuba divers with Lyme disease were being cured by doing deep dives. The deeper the diver went, the more nitrogen the body would pick up, and nitrogen killed bacteria. So I studied and trained and received my scuba certificate and traveled to New York and dove down one hundred-twelve feet. I do believe that God used many of these means to bring me to greater health and He taught me valuable lessons with each endeavor. Yet wouldn't the process, the journey have been so much more enjoyable if I could have shared it with God? Praying "Oh, God please make this work," more like a command and less like a participation in Father. Only beauty and grace will come from placing ands of our Lord and turning our trust to Him, who best of all. Truly trusting in God's will for our lives

the will of the
our life in the
knows our needs

means believing that God loves us and desires the best for us; faith at that level removes all anxiety. We realize that no matter how our lives turn out, God is there. It is going to be OK and His will prevails.

Just as anxiety and depression are partners in crime, trust and obedience are found eating together at the table of the Lord.

One of the facets of Aaron that I found fascinating was that in prison he was confident and I would even say secure. Even yet that still surprises me, and yet it is further evidence of Aaron's relationship with the Father. Aaron would write me encouragement as I worked on the book and as life trials came my way. He would say things like, "You are who God says you are, not who you tell yourself." I believe that is a statement that commands our introspection. I wonder how long it took Aaron to accept that. I was in my forties, people generally had a positive perspective of me, and I was still working on accepting that I was who God said I was and not who I was telling myself I was.

After thirteen years, Aaron's faith in God remained strong. Aaron wrote, "I'm still holding on to faith that I will walk out a scot-free man. Our Father will remove this reproach." Later he wrote, "My faith will carry me through. God knows the truth, he will deliver me." It is with trust and confidence that Aaron says, "Without my difficulties I wouldn't have testimony." I, too, have learned in my own life, as well as in those I meet, that it is the trials of life that give us character and define who we are. Will we be a person of hope, or will we be bitter and angry? At first it is a choice on our part, I believe, to accept the tragedies of our life; but when the tragedies and significant blows strike, it will be our faith that will hold us up. Only then in retrospect will we make the choice to allow that lowest moment to be our testimony. We can, of course, choose to have our trials define us or allow our testimony to shine. The wisdom of Proverbs 3:5–6 tells us: Lean not on your own understanding but acknowledge God in all your ways and he will direct your path. Once we fully accept the love of God, which I believe requires frequent affirmations on our trusting God becomes easier, because we accept that although beyond our human comprehension, God in his unchanging love us could only desire what is best for us. Anything else just wouldn make sense. If God loves us just as we are and desires what is best for us at all times, then our most logical conclusion is to put our trust in Him.

Perhaps as you read you may be inclined to think that Aaron is overly optimistic or is not seeing reality for what it really is. However, from my correspondence with him over three years, there were letters I received that reflected struggle. He wrote, speaking of being incarcerated, "It's hard, it's challenging, very exhausting mentally and spiritually draining." In that same letter he later writes, "I see God in the midst, I am aware of the hope inside my soul." As much as I wanted to believe that there was a fair and just system inside the prison, or that Aaron was safe and had access to help if he needed it, the reality was that he was living in an unpredictable, overstimulating and yet desolate place. I could be his friend, I could write him letters to encourage him and make him laugh, but I couldn't change his everyday harsh reality. Like Aaron, I had to accept that he was in prison, accused of a disgusting crime and there was nothing I could do about it but walk with him on this journey. Each of us know people we interact with, perhaps even daily, who have harsh realities that we cannot change, and yet we can choose to take the emotionally more challenging route and walk with them in their struggle, whether that be a friend with cancer, or a child with a learning disability, or someone with hidden wounds of past trauma. It is not easy to befriend the person in the middle of the storm or struggle, and yet when we are in the storm ourselves it is that one person who can be the difference between despair and hope, loneliness and love.

CHAPTER 24

FREEDOM AND JUSTICE
FOR SOME

A transformation in my outlook has occurred as I have gained experience. One of those many transformations is in the value of simple versus complex. As a child, the very best time of year was Christmas; it was so great that I always felt a little down the day after. My birthday was much the same. Over time, my most treasured holidays have been the simple ones. I love Easter because again we celebrate in unison the love of our God. As an American, the Fourth of July is always so very special. Nearly every year as I sit staring into the sky at the fireworks dazzling my eyes and the thunderous booms reverberating in my chest, an emotion of gratitude and pride swells within me causing tears to form. We truly live in an amazing country, most especially as women. Yet as amazing and as full of promise and opportunity as the United States is, the reality is that it does not provide equal opportunities for all.

July 4, 2017 was my first Fourth of July in Des Moines, Iowa. We had made the decision to move the previous year. We were settling into our new home and had made new friends and could now navigate around the city without GPS! So many triumphs! Des Moines turned out to be a wonderful location for our transracial family. Diversity was all around us. We had found places we blended in and truly each of the five of us was happy with our move, which was no easy accomplishment considering two of our daughters moved in middle school. We decided we would watch the fireworks right where all the action was, sitting on the lawn of the capital. Des Moines had quite a treat in store for us, as the Des Moines Symphony performed before and during the fireworks. The crowd was massive and yet the feeling of unity was palpable, most especially when we sang together and gasped in awe together. I could not help but to observe the various languages I heard around me; people from all races and walks of life.

As wonderful as it was sitting there, it was impossible not to think of those who lived right here among us and were not really free. Just barely two weeks earlier the Minnesota police officer who shot and killed Philander Castile was acquitted. A shocking and yet familiar verdict: Black man dead and no one to blame, at least no one who did the killing. There was always someone to blame, of course, the Black man himself. He was scary, he was running away, he was running toward, he was wearing the wrong clothing, he was outside after dark, he lived in the wrong neighborhood…so many reasons to blame. Mr. Castile seemed as though he would be different, perhaps I forgot that he was Black, or maybe I just held out hope that finally justice would be served and his life would matter enough. Perhaps it was the very notion that most of America had seen the bloody crime scene due to the live streaming of video of the crime by not only his girlfriend who was in the car, but also the police cam. Perhaps I thought that because everyone could clearly see that he was seat belted into the car, the very car in which the crime took place and the fact that a four-year-old child was in the backseat as a witness to this horrific shooting. Perhaps it was the fact that he was calm and clear and moved carefully explaining to the officer his every move, with clear, standard English. So the acquittal shook me to the core and flooded my mind and still lingered there over two weeks later as I watched the fireworks that Fourth of July.

I had visited Aaron just days before the fourth and it was impossible not to think of him and his loss of freedom. It was impossible not to acknowledge the skewed diversity I observed at the prison. Aaron had been transferred to another prison in the summer of 2017.

NOT surprisingly, this second prison in Illinois had the same racial imbalance as the previous. On my most recent visit to see Aaron, I noticed that all the inmates on visits who were Black were placed close to the desk of the correctional officer supervising the visits. I turned around to observe the room behind me, and to confirm my suspicion that those offenders behind me were white. Even in prison the surveillance of the Black man was at a higher level.

I am not sure I will ever visit a prison and not observe something new or gain a deeper understanding. Most recently, my visits to Aaron had given me exposure to some very young-looking inmates. They were skinny and lanky and looked more like they should be wearing the uniform of an after-school job or a team jersey running up and down a field rather than shuffling around in state-issued over-sized clothing. There was a noticeable difference in these young faces than the faces of older inmates: they looked lost. The older inmates always seemed to somehow be able to put on a brave or confident or accepting face, but the young inmates, they just looked lost. As the mother of a teenager, I wanted to mother them and solve their problems. As the mother of a teenager, I understood the quick and impulsive decision they may have made. I understood they likely had untrained tongues that were probably only a detriment to them when they were confronted by authority.

Yes, this was a great country, yes we had freedoms found nowhere else on the planet, but no, those freedoms were not for all. We professed and said we all had opportunities but the reality was that the road was much harder for some, and the surveillance was more intense for some. How could we change these cycles, these beliefs? How could we bring the topic to the forefront and seek a solution? That was likely a question we would still be asking in the future, but as for me I would do my best to stay attentive, not turn my eyes from injustice and speak up when needed. I would notice the privileges that I had that others did not, and I would make every attempt to balance the playing field so that we could all stand in unity and pride for this great country. I would refuse to believe that my ability to see inequality made me any less patriotic. In fact, it was the visionaries and those with a hope for something better who had drafted our constitution and dreamed of freedom. It was the spirit of hope that always moved us to a greater definition of what was encompassed in the title of "American."

CHAPTER 25

AT PEACE

Aaron writes, "This is not a story of an imperfect or perfect man, but a repented sinner who now calls Jesus his Lord and Savior, the Holy Spirit friend and comforter and the God of Heaven and Earth Yahweh, his Father."

"No doubt I've been through a lot, but it's like I was supposed to. So I wouldn't want it any other way. My life has been an interesting life, where I can say God is glorified and will continue to be glorified." Perhaps when we can all say that about our lives we will find the peace that Aaron has found, even if the world tells us differently, because we will then know that our value is not found in what others say, but rather our value is found in Jesus Christ. And when we humbly acknowledge that our value is found in Christ then we innately are aware that the value of our neighbor is found in Christ as well.

As I write these last sentences I realize that walking with another person is very different than solving their problem, implementing a strategy and making all well. Walking with someone is accepting their current situation, acknowledging the person's struggle and choosing to be a friend at a difficult time. Perhaps it is not how far we walk, or how many steps we take, but rather that we are willing to continue to put forth effort and have faith in God with each step we take. Is it possible that we can transform our world one friendship at a time? I say, yes, my friend, it is indeed!

ACKNOWLEDGMENTS

Aaron's Acknowledgements:

Thank you to my earthly mother and father for not aborting me.
My Heavenly Father, for my Savior Jesus.

Becky, for being Jesus in the flesh with love, mercy, and grace—
being mindful of me the least of these, as Jesus spoke of the repented
sinner.

To my children who give me a reason to continue on the path.

To my friend Cleve, you gave me hope when I needed it most.
I will never forget your determination to fight for justice when all
hope seemed lost. Thank you for inspiring me.

Finally, to my family, for there is no other like you, for real!

Becky's Acknowledgements:

Thank you to God Almighty for pursuing me and loving me
endlessly. I asked you for an adventure and you provided one I could
never have imagined.

To my husband, Pat, for his endless support and patience as I
wrote and immersed my life in this topic. Thank you for always loving me and always believing in me.

To my girls, the most enthusiastic cheerleaders a writer could
ask for and for making me look hard at myself and always pushing
me to do better.

To my friends Glenda, Cheng, and Angelina who prompted
and encouraged me to carry on writing and always believed in me.

Lastly, but most definitely not least, thank you to Aaron for
being willing to share your life story with me and the world. Your
courage and humility are inspiring. Thank you for being my friend
and accepting me as is…a work in progress.

REFERENCES

Alexander, Michelle. The New Jim Crow: Mass Incarceration in the Age of Colorblindness. New York: The New Press, 2012.

Cahill, Thomas. A Saint on Death Row: The Story of Dominique Green. New York: Nan A. Talese Doubleday Publishing Group, 2009.

Caron, Christina. Heather Heyer, Charlottesville Victim, Is Recalled as a Strong Woman. The New York Times. August 13, 2017. https://www.nytimes.com/2017/08/13/us/heather-heyer-charlottesville-victim.html

Esolen, Anthony. Magnificat. Year of Mercy Companion. New York: Magnificat Inc. 2016. Printed in Germany: CPI-Clausen & Bosse.

ESPN.com news services. Nelson Mandela's impact. ABC News. December 5, 2013. https://abcnews.go.com/Sports/nelson-mandelas-impact/story?id=21116739

Harris, Elise. 'To ignore the poor is to despise God,' Pope Francis says. Catholic News Agency. May, 18, 2016. https://www.catholicnewsagency.com/news/to-ignore-the-poor-is-to-despise-god-pope-francis-says-83026.

Ilibagiza, Immaculee with Erwin, Steve. Left to Tell: Discovering God Amidst the Rwandan Holocaust. Carlsbad, California: Hay House, Inc. 2006, 2014.

Jubilee of Mercy. Last updated November 20, 2016. https://www.im.va/content/gdm/en.html

Kelly, Matthew. Resisting Happiness. United States: Beacon Publishing, 2016.

King, Martin Luther Jr. The King Center. Accessed October 28, 2018. http://www.thekingcenter.org

Kochhar, Rakesh. How Americans compare with the global middle class. 2015. http://www.pewresearch.org/fact-tank/2015/07/09/how-americans-compare-with-the-global-middle-class/

National Human Genome Research Institute. Last updated September 7, 2018. http://www.genome.gov/19016904/faq-about-genetic-and-genomic-science/.

Nolan, Tony. Sermon. Winter Jam Concert. Des Moines, Iowa. 2017.

Paley, Frederick Apthorp. Greek Wit. 1881.

Parker, Billi-Jean. "Lion vs. Buffalo Epic Battle In An Epic War Documentary." May 12, 2015. National Geographic. https.//www.youtube.com/channel/UCZ855NcOAj_G266IW-IDYw

Picoult, Jodi. Small Great Things. New York: Ballantine Books, an imprint of Random House, a division of Penguin Random House LLC, 2016.

Rabin, Charles. Charles Kinsey was shot less than six minutes after police arrived. Miami Herald. August 5, 2016. https://www.miamiherald.com/news/local/crime/article94009242.html

Schmitz, Michael. Homily presentation, Christ Our Life Conference, Des Moines, Iowa, September 24, 2016.

Smith, Greg. Cross Burnings, Racist Actions Plague Dubuque. Associated Press. November 19, 1991. https://www.apnews.com/0fb49ca42aa6a51ac3f547608618849

Smith, Mitch. Minnesota Officer Acquitted in Killing of Philando Castile. The New York Times. June 16, 2016. https://www.nytimes.com/2017/06/16/us/police-shooting-trial-philando-castile.html

Weaver, Mike and Cowart, Benji. "Redeemed," Big Daddy Weave, (2012; Nashville, TN), http://www.metrolyrics.com/redeemed.lyrics-big-daddy-weave.html.

Wikipedia. Audrey Assad. Last updated October 2018. https://en.wikipedia.org/wiki/Audrey_Assad

Wikipedia. Black Lives Matter. Last updated October 2018. https://en.wikipedia.org/wiki/Black_Lives_Matter

Wikipedia. Chris Tomlin. Last updated October 2018.https.://en.wikipedia.org/wiki/Chris_Tomlin.

ABOUT THE AUTHOR

R.A. Naderman (Becky) studied at St. Ambrose University, graduating with a degree in occupational therapy and psychology. Her career as an occupational therapist has allowed her to encounter people from all walks of life. Becky resides in Des Moines, Iowa, with her husband and three daughters. *Walk with Me* is her first book. To contact Becky, email her at: RANaderman19@gmail.com

CPSIA information can be obtained
at www.ICGtesting.com
Printed in the USA
LVHW051032040720
659731LV00004B/389